BAD BRIDESMAID

BAD BRIDESMAID

Bachelorette Brawls and

Taffeta Tantrums

Tales from the Front Lines*

SIRI AGRELL

HENRY HOLT AND COMPANY

NEW YORK

*Names have been changed to protect the innocent (and the guilty).

Henry Holt and Company, LLC
Publishers since 1866
175 Fifth Avenue
New York, New York 10010
www.henryholt.com

Library of Congress Cataloging-in-Publication Data

Agrell, Siri.
   Bad bridesmaid : bachelorette brawls and taffeta tantrums—tales from
the front lines / Siri Agrell.—1st ed.
      p. cm.
   Contents: Prologue: disengaged—Engaged—Masturbating to Martha
Stewart—Sea foam blues—The golden shower—The bachelorette
complex—Extreme makeover—The big day—The honeymoon's
over—Epilogue: I do-over.
   ISBN-13: 978-0-8050-8269-2
   ISBN-10: 0-8050-8269-7
   1. Bridesmaids.   2. Wedding etiquette.   3. Weddings—Planning.
4. Bridesmaids—Humor.   5. Weddings—Humor.   I. Title.

BJ2065.W43A37 2007
395.2'2—dc22   2006051673

Henry Holt books are available for special promotions and
premiums. For details contact: Director, Special Markets.

First Edition 2007

Illustrations by Pepper Tharp

Designed by Kelly Too

Printed in the United States of America
1   3   5   7   9   10   8   6   4   2

To Gillian, for letting me be bad.

And Dave, for helping me be good.

CONTENTS

CHARLOTTE: I don't want to disappoint you, but I've decided not to have bridesmaids.

MIRANDA: Woohoo!

CARRIE: Hallelujah!

—*Sex and the City*

bad (băd)

1. Not achieving an adequate standard
2. Evil; sinful
3. Vulgar or obscene
4. Disobedient or naughty

brides·maid (brīdz'mād')

A woman who attends the bride at a wedding

bad bridesmaid (băd brīdz'mād')

An underachieving, inadequate, sinful, vulgar, naughty, or disobedient bridal attendant
Usually characterized by eye rolling, drunkenness, lack of pantyhose, and an overdrawn bank account

BAD BRIDESMAID

DISENGAGED

I can't believe it. You make someone a bridesmaid and they shit all over you.

—GINNY BAKER, *Sixteen Candles*

Call it a Bridesmaid Blindside.

It was late June, almost exactly one year since my friend had popped the question, asking me to be a member of her bridal party.

To be honest, I had never really considered myself bridesmaid material. I declined to play wedding dress-up as a child, and never hummed myself down an imaginary aisle with a pillowcase dangling from my head. I didn't take it upon myself to learn how to bustle a dress or clasp my hands properly around the stems of a bouquet. During most weddings, I pass the time fidgeting and taking pictures of my chest with the disposable cameras given to each table. In lieu of any useful advice or skills to offer as a bridesmaid, I spent our year of bridal preparations contributing in the only way I knew how: following people around, doing what I was told, and making a sarcastic comment whenever the opportunity presented itself.

When it was time for the bride and groom to register for gifts, I suggested the liquor store—an idea I personally believed to be genius—imagining nights spent sampling from the bottomless bar provided courtesy of their many wedding guests. When the couple instead chose to register at a more traditional retailer, I asked them to sign up for an espresso maker, which I could then purchase from them at a discounted price—another brilliant scheme for all involved. They didn't go for it.

Still, I found the whole process bizarrely entertaining, even though I was occasionally overwhelmed by the expense, excess, and drama of the bridal circus. I thought it was funny how much time, energy, and fifty-dollar-per-yard fabric could be employed in an event that would last a maximum of eight hours.

Little did I know, I was about to become the punch line in my own yearlong joke.

Twelve months of my life were filled with engagement celebrations, fittings, bachelorette parties, color consultations, band bookings, photographer selections, and premarital meltdowns. Like thousands of other women who are bridesmaids each year, I had bought gifts of racy lingerie and made an emotional speech. I had taken a cab to an undesirable part of town to have my hips measured at 8:00 a.m. by a Portuguese seamstress with little sympathy for my hangover or winter weight gain. I'd spent a hundred dollars on canapés to feed women who earn more than twice my salary, and spent a night lying on the cool tiles of my kitchen floor praying for death after drinking too much sangria at the shower.

All of these obligations were performed dutifully (if drunkenly) as I attempted to honor my close friend, who wanted her wedding tasteful and the lead-up textbook.

But a month before the wedding, I made a big mistake.

No, I did not sleep with the groom or let my ass spread beyond the contours accommodated by raw silk. I did not slap the soon-to-be mother-in-law or refuse to pony up for a hundred-dollar blow-dry. I simply asked why the bridesmaid's participation in all this pomp and circumstance was necessary—and I did it publicly.

In an article for a national newspaper, I admitted to being a Bad Bridesmaid, a woman who—while thrilled that her friend was engaged—could not get excited about the fine print. I had suggested the piece as part of a special section on weddings, and thought of it as a funny insider's look at being a bridal attendant. The job has evolved beyond ugly dresses and a solemn processional, I wrote, and into a commitment that borders on cultish.

I had been asked to be a bridesmaid by two friends that summer, and was surprised at just how much was really involved. When I started researching the bridesmaid institution, its origins and obligations, I was equally stunned by the advice given by wedding planners, etiquette experts, and seasoned attendants. Almost all of them acknowledged that being a bridesmaid is sometimes not a whole lot of fun, but the only response, they warned, is to shut up and take it.

"You might even be a hundred percent justified in wanting to have a scowl on your face for whatever it is you've been asked to do," said Joanna Dreifus, a woman who has served in so many weddings she founded the Web site Bridesmaid Aid (www.bridesmaidaid.com) with her friend Ellen Horowitz. "But a good bridesmaid will take the high road, let the bride have her day, and just complain about it behind her back."

Ridiculous, I thought. My friends are honest with one another, and that's why we remain so close. We have always been able to laugh at each other's bad habits, from our at times questionable taste in men to our unflagging commitment to overpriced clothes. My friends are not the kind of women who shy away from calling each other's bluffs or pointing out when one member of our group is being silly or unreasonable. And we almost always see eye to eye, agreeing on everything from vodka over gin to Owen Wilson over Luke. And so, when the first of our group became engaged, I like to think she selected the rest of us as bridesmaids because of who we are: women of independent means and a mean sense of independence.

Why, then, should being a bridesmaid have changed how I behaved around my friends?

My article hit newsstands while all of us were in the country for the bachelorette weekend. The bridal party had spent three blissful days drinking, eating, swimming, and lounging in a hot tub. We visited an antiques sale and danced in our bikinis when night fell, blasting the same JLo song over and over, a collection of deranged pseudo-strippers drunk on wine spritzers and our own supreme level of comfort among best friends. We debated the death penalty with the same vigor that we debated the pages of *Us Weekly* and whether celebrities were, in fact, just like us—returning to the city exhausted, tanned, happy, and viciously hungover.

Little did I know that weekend would be the last one I would spend as an honored member of the bridal party.

The next morning, I got an e-mail from The Bride. One of her co-workers had read my article and forwarded it to her electronically along with the message "I hope this isn't about you." She wanted to talk.

A week later, we both found time in our schedules, and I answered the Bridal Summons on a patio filled with first dates and après-work cocktailers. The air was redolent with lilac and smoke, and our rendezvous began as a rational conversation between two friends.

I was expecting her to tell me why she was upset about the article, which had mentioned a few scenarios lifted from her wedding preparation, each meant to highlight the importance of having a sense of humor when dealing with such a stressful event. I was fully prepared to defend my words and assure her that the article was in no way a personal attack.

As we sipped cocktails amid amorous couples, I explained that outing myself as a Bad Bridesmaid was a means to offer insight into a cultural phenomenon: the pressure that wedding attendants face while helping turn another woman's fantasy into reality. I told her that just because weddings were not my thing that didn't mean I didn't want to be a part of hers.

And then it happened.

"I just can't have any negative energy around my wedding," she said.

I was fired.

For a moment, it felt like a joke, as though I were being *Punk'd* or filmed for an episode of *Candid Camera*. There was no way someone would axe a bridesmaid for pointing out that her role was expensive and filled with stress. That would be like getting kicked out of Weight Watchers for admitting you were fat. I thought she was just trying to make a point—presenting the worst possible punishment so we could reach a compromise, where I would grovel and she would reclaim her Bridal Dominance. The worst-case scenario in my mind was having to shell out for an extra-nice wedding gift to make up for the perceived slight. Basically, I convinced myself that this could not possibly be happening.

"Don't make any decisions now," I begged her, promising that I would make amends, explain my position to her fiancé and family, and apologize to anyone else who'd thought I was poking fun at her rather than at the over-hyped ordeal of modern marriage ceremonies.

"You can do that if you want," she said, "but my cousin is wearing your dress."

My mind reeled. The Bride was someone I had always respected for the force of her convictions. She was the kind of woman who did not back down from a position once she had taken it, and I could tell by the tone of her voice that my expulsion from her wedding had never been an empty threat.

I flashed back to a phone call I'd made days earlier to reschedule a final dress fitting. Instead of suggesting an alternate date, the seamstress had stammered and stalled and finally suggested that I speak with The Bride, hanging up without offering me another appointment.

I realized then, sitting across the table from my friend as she sipped her drink and stared at me evenly, that a surly Portuguese grandmother had known I was eliminated from the bridal party before I did. Adding insult to injury, she had already pinned my dress on to my replacement's frame.

The Bride explained that her decision was not about our friendship, but about her wedding. She was calm and steely in her resolve. I spilled a drink and cried loudly. She said we could still be friends. I wondered if we ever really had been.

And with that, I was no longer a bridesmaid. I was a Former Bridesmaid. A Bad Bridesmaid. An ousted bridesmaid left pondering the remains of her friendship, her dignity, the last twelve months of her life, and approximately one thousand dollars of her recent earnings.

I walked the block back to my house in a state of shock. My boyfriend was on our patio with a group of male friends, enjoying nonconfrontational drinks.

"I'm out," I told them. "I'm out of the wedding."

They laughed hysterically and opened a bottle of wine. This was not a situation they would ever have to face. Men would never agree to wear matching lime green outfits in public—except possibly for hazing purposes.

Unlike them, however, I could not yet see the humor in my fall from grace. For weeks I would struggle with the implications of this incident on my friendship with The Bride and the other bridesmaids, and worry how it would affect the wedding and The Bride's mother, whom I adored and dreaded causing any further headaches. I felt terrible that an article intended to be funny had backfired so completely, and stung from the irony that I had rejected all the expert advice about biting my tongue, thinking such measures would not apply to my seemingly strong friendship.

My emotions ricocheted back and forth between feeling guilty for upsetting The Bride, and being amazed that she would reject my defense completely out of hand. I didn't know if she still wanted to be my friend, or if I still wanted to be hers. How could an eight-year friendship come to an end because I had made fun of bridesmaid dresses and the content of today's wedding registries? I felt like getting kicked out of a wedding had made me a social outcast or pariah, a woman who had scorned the wedding complex and felt its wrath in return.

Soon, my thoughts turned to the wedding itself, knowing I would still have to attend in two weeks' time, and I imagined walking into the ceremony marked with a scarlet *B*: for Bad, for Booted, for Bitch. It was too much to bear.

At first I told the other bridesmaids that I wasn't going, but eventually I swallowed my pride and fought off the sneaking suspicion that my friend had kicked me out of the wedding because I do not photograph well. I wondered how her cousin would feel seeing me in the audience, knowing that she was just a ringer and that she would have to shell out $250 for a dress designed for me.

On the Big Day, I forced myself to get dolled up and wrap the couple's wedding gift. I timed my day against theirs. As the bridal party was getting their hair done, I was eating bacon and reading the paper. As they left for the venue, I was sneaking an afternoon drink. While they helped The Bride get dressed, I was convincing myself to change out of sweatpants. I was scared, sad, and uncontrollably sweaty.

At last the time came to drive to the wedding, which was being held at a beautiful lakefront hunting club and golf course. My date and I pulled into the property, navigating slowly down the winding road surrounded by trees and immaculately manicured shrubbery. As we eased around a bend, an estate slowly came into view, as did—to my horror—the entire wedding party, who were standing on the driveway posing for photographs.

Clearly, we'd taken a wrong turn.

The only way back was to circle the roundabout in front of the club, a single lane now occupied by the bride, the groom, and their parents, plus three of my best friends and the pinch-hitting cousin, all dressed in identical green frocks and smiling happily—until we crashed the scene. Had I been behind the wheel, I would have slammed on the brakes, thrown the car into reverse, and accelerated backward across the eighteenth hole, through the surrounding forest, and all the way back to my apartment, where I would have lain in the bathtub with the shower on, drinking vodka out of the bottle and attempting to suppress the nightmare I had just experienced.

Unfortunately, I wasn't driving. My boyfriend, a far less dramatic individual and one merely amused by my personal torment, simply waited for the bridal party to step back onto the lawn and eased slowly past them as they stared at our bright red car. Like a bridesmaid version of *Invasion of the Body Snatchers*, I imagined them storming the vehicle as we drove by, a group of crazed wedding zombies beating the hood with their bouquets and stomping on the roof with their gold high heels, pointing at me and emitting a single blood-curdling scream that communicated to their alien wedding planner overlords: "She is not one of us."

In reality, the bridal party simply stood still and waited for us to go by. I resisted the urge to duck.

When we pulled into the parking lot at the other end of the proper driveway, I forced myself to get out of the passenger seat. Days before, I'd been convinced that attending would not be so bad, that I was a big enough person to walk into the wedding with my head held high. With just half an hour left until the ceremony, though, I wasn't sure if I could go through with it. Being a Bad Bridesmaid had made me feel like a lesser person, and an uninvited guest.

During the ceremony, the cousin who'd replaced me in the bridesmaid lineup kept looking my way, and I was sure she was taunting me, shoving my sins in my face with each glance in my direction. I fantasized about screaming that she was only in the wedding because I screwed up, knocking my chair over, tackling her to the floor, and ripping the bouquet from her hands. Then I realized that her boyfriend was sitting directly in front of me. It turns out she was smiling at him.

In the end, no one really seemed to notice me at all. The vast majority of the guests obviously had no idea they were looking at a Pinch-Bridesmaid, brought in during the late innings to relieve a player gone bad. They danced the night away, blissfully unaware of my shame and enjoying just another beautiful exchange of vows.

And a few hours later, it was all over. . . . Or so I thought.

During the weeks and months that followed, a steady stream of mail arrived in my inbox and my hands.

"I loved your article, I lived your article," wrote one woman.

"Thank you for finally coming clean about what being a bridesmaid means," read another e-mail. "Bridesmaids of the world unite!"

Soon, dozens more women had shared with me their tales of bridesmaid woe.

They e-mailed me about the dresses they were forced to wear that made them look like rejects from an eighties prom. I heard about women corralled into expensive last-minute spray-on tan sessions and doused with entire bottles of hair spray, with no regard for fire hazards or ozone depletion. I met bridesmaids who were bedazzled with glue-on jewels or asked to drive out of state to pick up the bride's dry cleaning while she relaxed on her honeymoon.

It became clear to me that bridesmaids had become collateral damage in the female quest for the perfect wedding.

My own wretched experience took on new life as an anecdote. I found myself encouraged to tell the story at parties, and listened to it being told for me at work. Every time I invoked my expulsion from the wedding party, someone else had an even better example of Bad Bridesmaid behavior. There was the girl who swore loudly during the ceremony, her blasphemy noticed by the priest and captured for posterity by the wedding videographer; and the two women who were kicked out of the same wedding after a last-minute makeup-related brawl, their hair already sculpted into place and with just hours remaining until the organ music accompanied the bridal party down the aisle.

There were women asked to stand up for virtual strangers or pissed off by flesh and blood. And in almost every closet there was still a three-hundred-dollar floor-length, puffy-sleeved dress with an empire waistline and panels of flame-retardant fabric that some poor girl had been forced to wear.

I was not alone.

Bad Bridesmaids are everywhere. We are getting our hair twisted in unflattering updos with wispy ringlets framing our faces, and pulling on control-top panties in eighty degree heat. We are trying to rent stretch Hummers in towns so small they don't even have a Starbucks, and taking calligraphy classes so we can help the bride personally pen 250 invitations. Some of us are wondering why we haven't been asked to stand up for our best friends, or are contemplating stepping down altogether. Others will soon hit the dance floor in strapless dresses, praying that their breasts will be restrained as they hop their way through another embarrassing rendition of the Chicken Dance. And somewhere, for the very first time, a woman is seeing the glint of a diamond reflected in her best friend's eyes and wondering what exactly she has gotten herself into.

In the name of making another woman's dream day come true, bridesmaids swallow a lot along with their free champagne. We risk losing our dignity, our credit ratings, our natural waistlines, and—sadly—even our friends.

And in return, we don't get a ring, a honeymoon, or even a china pattern to call our own. But there is something every bridesmaid does have: a story.

It is the tales of bachelorette brawls and taffeta tantrums that unite us in our shared experience, and make the months of wedding work almost worthwhile. The bride may have months to orchestrate her wedding, but bridesmaids get the rest of their lives to dine out on stories of how it all went down.

So let her toss the bouquet. It's time for us to dish the dirt.

1

ENGAGED

You should select bridesmaids who are reliable, flexible, and available to help with the details and planning of your wedding. It also helps if your chosen bridesmaids are happy for you, instead of having feelings of jealousy that may be revealed in a passive aggressive manner.

—GAYLE O'DONNELL, *A Perfect Celebration!*

My friend had just returned from France with a large princess-cut diamond and a tentative July wedding date a year away when she announced the lineup of her bridal attendants. Along with her older brother—who would be her suit-wearing Maid of Honor—there were to be four of us bridesmaids, close friends who had been in one another's lives for almost a decade. Like refugees from *Sex and the City*, we were a mixed bag of personalities linked by our recent history, common interests, and frequent bouts of hysterical laughter. For us, being asked to be in The Bride's wedding party was as natural as deciding to go for dinner or skip out early from work to meet for a drink (which we did to celebrate her engagement), and we slid easily into roles befitting the peculiarities of our characters.

There was Kind Bridesmaid, a woman who even cries during sitcom weddings; Super Bridesmaid, capable of whipping up a four-course gourmet meal with the ease most women reserve for breathing; and Experienced Bridesmaid, who had stood up for so many of her friends that she could outfit a small rainbow-colored army with her collection of floor-length formal wear.

I liked to think of myself as Comic Relief Bridesmaid. I don't tear up during toasts, but I mix a mean martini and can find an inappropriate joke where others see only harmony and bliss. I had never been a bridesmaid before and wasn't banking on being asked, my personal strengths being more conducive to ending marriages than helping them prosper. When the time came, however, I found myself reverting to the logic of playground philosophy: crossing my fingers and hoping to be picked.

In this way, the bridesmaid draft occurs in fits and starts throughout the year. Upon the gushing news of each engagement, relatives and girlfriends hold their collective breath until the chosen ones are named. And just like it is when kids select their grade-school dodgeball teams, the process isn't always fair.

PARADISE LOST

Sarah G. met Michelle on the beach. Both women were on vacation with their respective boyfriends, spending a week relaxing at a tropical resort. Their whirlwind friendship began when the two couples realized that they came from the same city, a happy coincidence in a faraway land. They struck up a conversation and soon were meeting for dinner, hanging out on the sand, and sipping cocktails together poolside—double-dating vacation-style. When the holiday was over, the couples promised to stay in touch, and Michelle called Sarah within weeks to make plans to meet for coffee.

"A few months later she called again," Sarah said.

This time, Michelle announced that she was engaged and informed Sarah that she would be a bridesmaid at the wedding. "I didn't even have a chance to say anything; it was just done," the stunned recruit remembered. "All I was thinking was, 'You don't even know me.'"

They'd spent only a handful of days together, but Sarah and her boyfriend were both included in the couple's wedding party. For the next year, Sarah attended multiple showers where she knew no one but The Bride. She bought a two-hundred-dollar dress that she hated and literally threw in the garbage the night after the wedding. And for a brief period, Sarah allowed the groom-to-be to camp out in the house she and her boyfriend had just bought. The engaged couple's own home was under renovation, so while his fiancée moved back in with her parents, the groom persuaded his new friends to clear off their couch. What was supposed to be a brief sleepover turned into weeks of house-guest horror, and while the bride and groom lived for free, Sarah and her boyfriend shelled out for engagement gifts, a Vegas bachelor party, and wedding presents, even as they struggled to make their own mortgage payments.

When the day of the wedding finally arrived, Sarah and her boyfriend looked around at a room filled with strangers. They were seated at a head table where no one knew their names and spent the majority of the evening picking fights with one another so they would have an excuse to lash out. The rubbery meal and token gifts they received did little to offset their investments or their moods.

"We were both like, 'What are we doing here?'" Sarah remembered. Their one-week vacation in paradise had turned into a thousand-dollar year from hell.

An American bride selects, on average, five women to stand at her side during her wedding ceremony, meaning that there are about eight million attendants recruited each year. This is enough women to tip the balance in a presidential election or to invade and conquer a midsize nation with one hand tied behind their Pilates-toned backs.

Few brides-to-be have five women in their family, though, so this army of attendants is drafted from the ranks of cousins, friends, co-workers, and sometimes even casual acquaintances.

Lindsay D. was once asked to be a bridesmaid for a woman she had cast in a short film the year before. "I had sort of kept in touch with her afterward, in a professional kind of way," she remembered.

The Bride had since moved from Canada to the States, and the wedding was to be held in Palo Alto, California. Lindsay cobbled together the airfare, as well as money for the dress and alterations, a commitment she would soon regret. During the ceremony, she was glared at by The Bride when she tried to take the bouquet at the wrong time and was told afterward that she could buy a copy of the wedding video or individual photographs for twenty-five dollars apiece. It would be her only experience as a bridesmaid, and she would never quite figure out why she had put herself through it.

"But," she reasoned years later, "I was the one who said yes."

It is almost impossible to refuse a bridesmaid invitation, regardless of whether the bride is your arch nemesis or your conjoined twin. Books of bridal etiquette encourage women to select attendants who will be obedient, helpful, punctual, and above all, grateful to be a part of it—like sorority rushes begging to be ridiculed for their baby fat while vying desperately for a collection of new best friends.

Sarah G. said she agreed to be in the wedding of the woman she met on vacation because The Bride's excitement was contagious, and she didn't want to ruin the moment.

"I thought, 'Well, if you think I'm *that* nice, I don't know . . . .' I like people to think I'm nice," she said. "Not anymore, though."

LADIES IN HATING

The Original Bridesmaids were selected not because they were nice but because they were disposable. Servants or sisters, concubines or commoners, bridesmaids were meant to be decoys from the main attraction. The institution began, like many doomed displays of power, in Roman times. Back when every day was a toga party, bridesmaids served as a protective shield, accompanying the bride to the ceremony and prepared to intervene—with their presumably dainty fists—if anyone made a move to kidnap her or steal her dowry.

Many brides were barely teens when they were led down the aisle, and bridesmaids were also there to dress them, instruct them in the ways of "pleasing" their new husband, and ensure that they didn't bolt before taking their vows.

When bridesmaids of yore weren't thwarting crime or babysitting the bride, they were upholding societal standards in a more basic way, acting as witnesses to the marriage itself. Roman law required that every wedding have ten witnesses, the historic precursor to today's absurdly large bridal parties. Everyone knows you can't build Rome in a day, but some women think they can re-create the customs of the late empire while exercising their marital might. And many brides take on the air of Cleopatra from the very beginning.

"She was so excited about being waited on hand and foot that in her head it was like becoming the queen," Rosie G. said about the friend for whom she was a bridesmaid. "She really saw her bridesmaids as people working for her. We were staff. In her mind she had constructed it as this perfect event, with her bridesmaids carrying her on their shoulders."

The underlings of a blessed union should be prepared not just to honor and obey their bride but also to contend with one another. Every bridal party has a pecking order, and more often than not that pecking can escalate into full-blown bitch-slaps.

Wendy H. was asked to be a bridesmaid seven times in one year while she was still in college, and despite the obligations to her studies, she said yes to all of them: high school friends, college friends, even distant relatives. Out of all of the weddings, she dropped out of only one: that of her best friend from grade school.

Wendy had been asked to be Maid of Honor, the senior member of a bridal party that also included a woman named Rachel, whom she totally despised. A month into the wedding plans, Wendy began to feel like the other bridesmaid was sabotaging her every move. Unhappy that she was not the Maid of Honor, Rachel was going out of her way to make Wendy appear incompetent and was positioning herself as the heiress apparent, a Shakespearean villain for the H&M set. "She kept suggesting all these weird things, like trips to Mexico that she knew I couldn't take while I was in school," Wendy said. Eventually, The Bride suggested that Wendy relinquish her duties all together, passing the MOH torch to Rachel.

"She basically moved in with her," Wendy said of the conniving co-attendant. "And I couldn't drop everything to drive across the country looking for these odds and ends." Wendy gave up the gig and was recast as a lowly bridesmaid, but things within the bridal party did not improve.

"I just couldn't get along with Rachel, and it made me feel like I had nothing in common with The Bride," she said. "Between the two of them I didn't even want to go to the wedding anymore."

Her breaking point came at the bridal shower, when Rachel hired a stripper to attend along with The Bride's grandparents and various impressionable children. The surreal scene was too much for Wendy to take, and she told her friend she was leaving. The Bride cautioned her that exiting the event early would buy her a one-way ticket out of the wedding party, but Wendy took one look at the naked man gyrating around Granny's lap and fled.

Unfortunately for bridesmaids like Wendy, there is no prenuptial agreement between friends, no guarantee that you will recover your losses if things go wrong during the wedding, and no makeup sex after a particularly nasty argument has you lunging for each other's throats. And yet bowing out *before* things get ugly is nearly impossible if you want to stay friends with the bride. Ironic, isn't it?

Rebecca L. was asked to be a bridesmaid for a friend and roommate, a woman with such a commanding personality she would make Madonna seem demure. Despite her visions of losing a relationship and a rent-controlled apartment if things went wrong, Rebecca couldn't imagine saying no.

"I thought it would cause friction, and I would still be hearing about her wedding all the time anyway," Rebecca said. "I thought the easier path to take would be to just grit my teeth and do it." After two weeks, however, it was clear she had not selected the path of least resistance. The Bride had become so demanding that other members of the bridal party were trying to back out, with one woman telling her, "If I stay a bridesmaid, we won't be friends."

It seemed like a rational thing to admit, but The Bride would not let the woman go that easily. She cried and sent the bridesmaid flowers, adopting the tone and technique of an abusive husband promising that things would be different the second time around.

"Basically she wooed her back," Rebecca said.

After the first failed escape, two more bridesmaids decided to run the gauntlet, hoping at least one of them would make it out alive. At a planned sit-down, they suggested that The Bride's vision of a classy black-tie wedding would be better served if she just had one bridesmaid, her sister.

"She didn't buy that, either," sighed Rebecca, who ended up walking down the aisle as part of a completely intact, if not altogether willing, bridal party.

Even legitimate excuses like expense, distance, and work can fail to impress a bride in need of bridesmaids, or release a girl from the shackles of servitude.

"I had a girlfriend who was sort of iffy about coming in from Australia," remembered three-time bridesmaid Tamara B. The plane ticket alone would have cost the woman $2,500, an expense she was not prepared to incur.

"All of a sudden, because she had been anointed bridesmaid, it was like, 'What do you mean you're not going to spend that money?'" Tamara said, recalling The Bride's reaction. The woman remained Down Under despite the Bridal Ultimatum, and the friendship between them soon headed south as well.

WHITE WOOING

If women cannot decline even the most unexpected or far-afield invitation, imagine how hard it must be to say no when seduction is in play. The modern bride now sees each element of her engagement as an opportunity to acquire the best, and is ready to do almost anything to get what she wants. From an ice sculpture shaped like a childhood pet to a kindergarten friend flown in from Siberia to waltz down the aisle, if the bride wants it, it will be hers.

Cele Otnes, co-author of *Cinderella Dreams: The Allure of the Lavish Wedding*, says that brides regard their bridesmaids as one more part of the wedding to customize, and they soup up their friends like a human version of *Pimp My Ride*.

"The more attendants, the more lavish," Otnes says. "If you're really going to have a perfect, luxury-laden day, everybody's got to buy into it."

Taking a page from the awkward and acne-riddled twenty-first-century teenage boys who use balloon-o-grams and midnight serenades to beg out-of-their-league girls to accompany them to the prom, some women have invented elaborate methods of adding pizzazz to the bridesmaid selection process.

Three-time bridesmaid Jenny T. claims that straightforward inductions into bridal parties are now a thing of the past among her friends. They've stopped picking up the phone like normal human beings and have begun issuing formal invitations, each one with an increasingly outlandish presentation. One bride showed up at Jenny's door with a poster that she had decorated with photographs of the two of them over the years, taken everywhere from childhood sleepovers to college keg parties. She had laminated it like a freakish eighth-grade art project, and written a personalized poem of rhyming couplets that told the story of their relationship and asked, in the final stanza, for Jenny to be a bridesmaid.

It might have gone a little something like this:

We met, my friend, as little girls,
Our socks worn high, our hair in curls.
In high school, yes, we grew apart,
You laughed when Adam broke my heart.
The cool kids called you, I felt their wrath.
You drank in parks, I studied Plath.
Who's laughing now, my former pal?
I'm getting hitched, you single gal.
So put on this dress, a lavender bomb.
You'll be my bridesmaid, or I'll tell your mom.

Okay, so maybe not exactly like that. But it rhymed, and the Poet Bride had written one for each of her fourteen chosen friends.

"Then she presented us with four yards of fabric for the dresses," said Jenny. "I thought it was a joke."

The lengths some women will go to in the name of building the perfect wedding party are deadly serious. In the world of celebrity, where excess is the name of the game, brides are capable of putting as much cash and firepower into their weddings as the average Spielberg flick. For her much-discussed 2004 nuptials, former talk show host Star Jones was preceded down the aisle by three matrons of honor, twelve bridesmaids, two junior bridesmaids, and four flower girls. The women she chose were friends, but were also conveniently assembled from an all-star cast of prominent Americans including Vivica A. Fox, Natalie Cole, and Karenna Gore Schiff, daughter of former Vice President Al Gore and the only member of that family to successfully lead any party, bridal or otherwise.

Such Bridal Casting is not unusual, even for less diva-ish brides. Selecting impressive or attractive women to be in your wedding tells people that you, too, are impressive and attractive, and some brides even recruit long-lost friends from grade school or camp to act as living, breathing, bad-dress-wearing tributes to the different stages of their lives.

Another of Jenny T.'s friends created personalized jogging outfits for her crew of bridesmaids, an effort to brand them well in advance of the big day. Each woman's name was printed on a jacket and matching tee, with the word *bridesmaid* emblazoned on the bum—an attendant uniform for her team of wedding cheerleaders.

"We had to wear them at every wedding-related activity," Jenny T. said ruefully. "It was meant to bring us together."

Sadly, just because a bride has a brigade of strong women outfitted with gifts and gym gear, it does not mean they will work in harmony. Jenny said that most of the velour-wearing bridesmaids in her wedding party were barely speaking to one another by the time the wedding was over. And the outrageous demands made by Star Jones reportedly alienated her longtime friends and sparked an East Coast/West Coast feud between factions of the bridal party. Thankfully the wedding ended before we had another Biggie/Tupac situation on our hands.

KNOCKED UP AND KNOCKED OUT

There is only one excuse that seems to fly when it comes to bowing out of a bridal party, and it has nothing to do with losing your tracksuit or being called away to film *Kill Bill: Vol. 2*. In the hierarchy of female achievement, bearing a child trumps having a wedding—and no woman wants to be shown up on Her Day.

Brides will almost always release their pregnant friends from wedding obligations if they are worried about losing the spotlight, as people tend to find pregnant bellies even more hypnotic than large diamond rings. And God forbid the bride's moment of glory is eclipsed by a surprise delivery halfway down the aisle.

Mary G. was three months pregnant when her two cousins, Liz and Melissa, descended on her doorstep for a girls' weekend. Mary was the first of them to get knocked up, and her sister, Jane, had planned a fun weekend of baby talk and shopping. Liz, however, soon announced that she was engaged, and the conversation turned from babies to bridesmaids. She asked all three women to be in the wedding the following May, a date just three months after Mary's baby would be born.

"I was due in February, so the jokes started about me being the bridesmaid with porn star nursing boobs," Mary said. "Then Liz tells Jane and Melissa that they are *not allowed* to get pregnant between now and the wedding, as she doesn't want any pregnant bridesmaids."

Awkwardly enough, it turned out that Jane had just found out that she was expecting, and was due two weeks before Liz's wedding date. When she owned up to her status, you'd think it would have been cause for even more celebration. But instead of being happy for her cousin, Liz started to wonder aloud whether the bun-in-the-oven bridesmaid would be able to fulfill her duties.

"There was a lot of back-and-forth about the subject, and in the end Liz made it subtly obvious that perhaps Jane should bow out of the wedding party."

By the time Jane did offer to step down, Liz had

already lined up her sister-in-law as a replacement, but she could not rein in her own sister's libido.

"Her sister Melissa ended up being an eight-month-pregnant Maid of Honor." Mary laughed. "A little karma, I suppose!"

You know we have reached the point of Bridesmaid Overload when getting pregnant seems like a reasonable course of revenge.

OVERLOOKED AND UNDERTAKEN

Remember seven-timer Wendy H.? Even after years of insisting she'd never agree to be a bridesmaid again, she admitted that she was hurt when a close friend didn't ask her to join the party. "There was just this tiny feeling in the beginning of 'We're really good friends; why didn't she just ask me?'" she said. "I kept waiting and waiting when I kind of knew it was coming, and then when it didn't happen, part of me was really put out."

The Bride knew about her friend's storied bridesmaid past, but Wendy had made it clear she would participate in another wedding if it was for a close friend. She began to worry that her friend didn't understand how she felt, or worse, that maybe they weren't as close as she had thought. In fact, The Bride eventually admitted that her bridal party was being carefully constructed through tense family negotiations, over which she had very little sway.

"She told me that because of expectations from [the groom's] family, if she invited someone like me to be in the wedding party, they would expect her to include other people that they know," Wendy said.

Anteing up to have her friend in the wedding would have caused The Bride's mother-in-law to increase the stakes with a second cousin or a freakish family friend. It was a game of premarital poker, and Wendy's friend had folded at the first bridal party bluff.

Deborah McCoy, a wedding planner in Boca Raton, Florida, and president of the American Academy of Wedding Professionals, says women are inviting lots of bad karma in the way they choose their bridesmaids. She advocates selecting only immediate family members and close friends, and women who have the means to finance the bride's desires.

"It's not fair to ask people to spend an exorbitant amount of money on your wedding and also expect them to give you a gift and an engagement gift and a shower gift and every other gift," she said. "It creates a great amount of tension."

McCoy says she is constantly advising brides about picking their parties, but her words are rarely heeded, especially when she warns against adding to the numbers just to perfect the male/female ratio.

"If your fiancé has six groomsmen and you only have five bridesmaids, leave it," she says. "Don't invite somebody to even up the numbers, because that person will come back to haunt you. Because they know it."

One such bridesmaid walked into a Toronto boutique last year, said Danielle V., a seamstress who specializes in custom-made designs. "I had been making bridesmaid dresses for six women, and this one name had changed three times," she said. When the mystery bridesmaid turned up in the store, Danielle was surprised by her surly attitude toward the dress and the wedding as a whole, and eventually asked the woman if she was close with the bride. She was surprised to hear, "Actually, I thought we were best friends." The disgruntled bridesmaid had chosen the current bride-to-be to serve as her own Maid of Honor, and assumed that there would be reciprocation of roles when her friend got engaged.

But she was not one of the six original bridesmaids named. The Bride had only one sister, so it was not as if the would-be BFF was passed over due to family obligations. Offered no role or explanation, she was left to nurse her wounded ego until one of the chosen bridesmaids discovered that she was pregnant. It turned out that the expecting attendant's due date coincided almost exactly with the wedding day, and she knew the tight satin dress would never accommodate her swelling belly.

Again there was an opening for a bridesmaid and again the hopeful (but increasingly irate) friend was passed over. By this point, the woman had mentally crossed The Bride off her list of friends and was trying to decide what movie she would go see on the day of the wedding, instead of sitting in the pews as a two-time reject.

"And then—and this is awful," recalled Danielle, "but another girl in the bridal party actually died."

The Bride finally contacted her twice-passed-over friend and asked her to sub-in for the passed-away member of the bridal party, informing her that she had a similar body shape to that of the deceased.

"It wasn't even like she was next in line. She was the friend who was closest to the dead girl's size," Danielle said. "She was literally filling a dead girl's shoes."

LARGEST GATHERING OF OVERDRESSED STRANGERS

For one bride, the dearly departed were the only ones who escaped a bridesmaid designation. When Christa Joachim married her husband, Suresh, in 2003, she had seventy-nine bridesmaids walk her down the aisle and into the *Guinness World Records*.

"It was my husband's idea," she said.

Christa had fallen for a man who loved breaking records almost as much as he loved her. He had broken more than twenty-seven *Guinness* records and hoped that his wedding would win him three more. Relieved, perhaps, that he had not opted to grow the world's longest toenails or become the fattest man alive, Christa got married with the most bridesmaids, the most groomsmen (forty-seven), and the longest bouquet (197 feet 1 inch), a category that defies all logic and explanation. Christa said she knew only about half of her bridesmaids, and considered a mere half dozen actual friends. The rest she had culled from the neighborhood and through word of mouth, outfitting each in a matching red sari that, by *Guinness* rules, the couple was forced to pay for—also putting them in the running for the world's largest monthly Visa statement.

"I asked co-workers and then they asked their friends and relatives," Christa said of her bridesmaid-selection process. "It was neighbors, it was everyone." The youngest bridesmaid was eighteen months and the oldest was seventy-nine years old. At least those two probably got to sleep through most of the ceremony.

MY BEST FRIEND'S WETTING

There are no etiquette books that discuss whether it is worse to ask every person you know to be in your wedding, or none of them. In 2005, a British woman named Sonia Wile opted for the latter option and sought permission from her local vicar to have her dog, Lucy, act as her one and only bridesmaid. It was unusual for an animal to participate in a religious rite, but the church eventually granted permission for the pooch to make its way down the aisle.

"I can't think of anybody else I would rather have as a bridesmaid," she told the media at the time. "Lucy's my best friend, and you want the people you love by your side on the big day."

Obedient, faithful, and willing to wear mauve chiffon, Lucy may just have been the perfect bridesmaid. It's no surprise, then, that Sonia is not the only woman to pass over friends and family for her furry friend. Designers have even started to sell bridesmaid dresses for bulldogs and tuxedoes for terriers, outfitting pets for their owners' big days. For her million-dollar wedding, Tori Spelling had her puppy as a bridesmaid. Too bad the marriage didn't last long, even in dog years.

It may be depressing to see a place of matrimonial pride occupied by a creature that will probably mark its territory as the bride kisses the groom. But I, for one, take comfort in the fact that I'm not the only bitch who's ever been in someone's wedding.

2

MASTURBATING TO MARTHA STEWART

As your wedding day approaches, demands on your time will be great. On the following pages we give you a personal calendar where you can fill in appointments month by month, week by week, and finally, hour by hour.

—*The Wedding Planner,* by Martha Stewart

Like many modern-day deviants, it was the Internet that first led me astray. I received my initial Bad Bridesmaid designation months before being kicked out of the actual bridal party, after posting a message on The Bride's self-created wedding Web site.

According to Peggy Post's *Wedding Etiquette*, bridesmaids are expected to understand their duties, follow instructions, and "arrive at specified times for all wedding-related events." In reality, though, the average engagement period in the United States is now 17 months long, and bridesmaids are actively involved from the moment the ring is appraised to the last nibble of mini-quiche at the post-wedding brunch.

In between, there are meetings, consultations, lunches, and field trips. Magazines are dispensed and pages earmarked, brides and their friends single-handedly supporting the market for pink Post-it notes and prescription uppers. Today, bridal parties must not only sign the wedding Web site, but also help decide whether there will be a martini bar or champagne fountain, fireworks or smoke machines, Bible verse or Beyoncé song. For the bridesmaids, indoctrination is swift and merciless, and attendants are expected not just to help out with that one day, but rather to commit as much time and effort as one would to the average undergraduate course or rehab program. And I've never been one for studying or sobriety.

Months before my bride's wedding, she e-mailed her attendants instructing us to sign the guest book on her Web site immediately, an Internet oasis of love where her engagement photo glistened beside a handy link to her registry. Her grandparents had already checked in, and it would be bad form if more guests logged on to the site before The Bride's own trusted bridesmaids left their mark.

It was not a major request, granted, but I could not bring myself to do it with a straight face. I had clipped pictures of dresses I liked to bring to a wedding party working lunch, and had discussed the various pros and cons of indoor versus outdoor ceremonies. But typing my name into her guest book seemed forced and silly, with no real payoff, like leaving a message on a movie star fan site or forwarding an e-mail in the hopes that a Nigerian refugee would immediately deposit a million dollars into my checking account.

I read the other bridesmaids' sincere missives: "So excited!" and "Can't wait til the big day!" Part of me wished I could write something kind and unsarcastic like that, but a larger part found it strange that after months of tangibly demonstrating our excitement, we were also expected to release our joy into cyberspace, a realm I believe should be reserved purely for pornography, eBay, and videos of young men doing incredibly stupid things. So instead of simply signing my name, I opted for a joke.

"I give it six months," I typed, beginning my Bad Bridesmaid career in earnest, then added: "Just kidding. So excited."

After months of wedding party training, I had not yet learned that when it comes to assigned tasks, bridesmaids have little room for improvisation. It was the beginning of the end of my stand-up wedding career.

DR. JEKYLL AND MRS. BRIDE

Being involved in every aspect of bridal planning can take an emotional toll on women who do not know how to help, or who don't care to be of much assistance in the first place—the hallmarks of a Bad Bridesmaid's character.

Many attendants develop a ringing in their ears from the constant white noise of wedding chatter, and find it difficult to weigh in on whether Mariah Carey's "Vision of Love" makes a better first-dance song than Josh Groban's "You Raise Me Up," if in fact they can listen to either without instantly developing diabetes.

Offering advice to friends in the midst of major life decisions is never easy, even when the results will not be judged by two hundred guests and the couple's chosen deity. If you tell your girlfriend that her live-in lover is an asshole, chances are they'll be engaged within the year. Give a bride a definitive opinion on anything from hair to heirloom jewelry, and you're just begging for a Bridal Backhand.

Francine K., a four-timer, had just returned home from work one night when her friend The Bride called her from a wedding boutique, crying. She had found a wedding dress that she loved but required a second opinion before deciding if it was The One.

"She absolutely *needed* me to come and give my opinion, because she knew I would be honest and the decision had to be made that night," Francine remembered. "It was this whole big thing. So of course I went down." So far, Good Bridesmaid.

There was added urgency to the mission because another bride-to-be had tried on the dress in question earlier that day, and was returning the next morning for a "second visit." Convinced it would soon be snatched up, Francine's friend had refused to take the gown off until her bridesmaid appeared, the wedding equivalent of Charlton Heston declaring his weapons could be pried from his "cold dead hands"—only, in this case, the dress would have been clutched in a death grip featuring a lovely French manicure.

When Francine got to the store, The Bride was standing in front of a full-length mirror in a stunning raw silk strapless gown, fending off other brides with death stares and nervous energy. The dress was a sample from an as-yet-unreleased designer line, the bodice ruched and gathered dramatically at the waist and the flowing skirt bias cut and swept into a long, elegant train. It was everything The Bride had described in the frequent and detailed discussion of her dream dress.

"'It is absolutely beautiful, and if you want my opinion on this you have to buy this dress immediately,'" Francine said, believing that she was performing her role to a tee.

It seemed like a no-brainer. Her friend was standing there in a one-of-a-kind creation that few people in the world had even seen. Because it was a sample and could not be ordered to measure, its normal price of seven thousand dollars had been reduced to just two thousand, and it was perfect for her price range and her body. What else should The Bride have said but, "Wrap it up. I'll take it"?

This Bride, however, had another plan. She opened the door to the dressing room to point out a pile of other dresses she wanted to try on in front of her friend. It was almost 9:00 P.M., and the store was closing, but Francine sat patiently (Good Bridesmaid) and looked at each dress in turn. With all the dresses modeled, she once again offered her opinion that the first dress was definitely the way to go. Instead of agreeing and thanking her friend for the reassurance, The Bride burst into a fresh round of tears and started berating her bridesmaid in front of the store employees and other customers, screaming at her for being too opinionated.

"She flipped out and said I was pressuring her into making a decision she wasn't ready to make," said

Francine, now firmly entrenched in the ranks of Bad Bridesmaids worldwide. With a pile of expensive white fabric at her feet, and a boutique full of employees and engaged women looking on, The Bride launched into a fit of sobbing invective directed at her stunned attendant.

One might think a woman sporting a diamond ring and a full-length white silk gown would be all about making lifelong decisions. Hardly. Much to Francine's shock and dismay, she was loudly informed that the proper course of action would have been to avoid passing judgment on the initial dress and suggest instead that her friend try on a few more, commenting on how beautiful each of them looked and then gently steering her back to the original.

Such mind games should be covered in *Modern Bride* magazine, and taught in Psych 101.

The women left without the dress, and on the way home The Bride told Francine that she had always imagined trying on wedding gowns while her friends and family sipped tea from delicate china cups and told her how lovely she looked, their eyes lighting up when she emerged in The Dress. Effectively, The Bride concluded, Francine had crushed her lifelong dress-buying dreams.

The next day, The Bride called to say she had bought the dress after all, that once she was away from her friend's "pressure" she realized it was in fact the one for her. "She asked me to come to the first fitting," Francine recalled. "I wholeheartedly declined."

NOT-SO-GREAT EXPECTATIONS

Until the early twentieth century, wedding preparations were a relatively simple affair, with brides concentrating on their hope chests and whether conjugal bliss would prove all it was cracked up to be, while the menfolk tended to the pesky details such as who would be marrying whom and in exchange for how many chickens.

Like an out-of-control flesh-eating virus, the wedding world has since expanded into a billion-dollar industry that threatens to swallow us all, and new products, services, and standards emerge on an almost daily basis to further complicate the lives of blushing brides and their sweating servants.

Most women do not inflict unfair demands on their bridesmaids because they are naturally cruel or unfeeling, but rather because they have been conditioned to believe that their wedding will reflect their personal worth and predict the happiness of their future marriage. It's not the brides who are crazy, for the most part, but the expectations placed upon them.

One issue of *Martha Stewart Weddings*, for example, encourages brides to make their own origami boxes as wedding favors and to develop a "signature drink" for their wedding reception. The pages that follow further sing the praises of hiring a calligrapher to pen the wedding invites or learning to write the cumbersome curlicues oneself.

That ought to be enough to keep a bride and her maids busy for the duration of the engagement, but the magazine has a few more tricks up its cashmere sleeve. There is a recipe for homemade meringue kisses, and for the seaman's bride, Martha provides four variations of knots to use when hand-tying your own napkin rings. One page shows how to make egg hors d'oeuvres and arrange them in handwoven basket centerpieces. Another features homemade ribbon boutonnieres, table runners crafted from wrapping paper, and clever save-the-date cards, where the numbers are individually cut out and attached to a ribbon so they tumble to the floor like confetti when the envelope is opened. There are also five pages on how to select your china, and a guide for constructing bouquets entirely out of tissue paper. Amazingly, the magazine stops short of having wedding parties swear blood oaths or carve the happy couple's like-nesses from stone using only their fingernails and a melon-baller—but maybe they are saving that for the next issue.

For those who do not have a degree in home economics and an up-to-date Xanax prescription, these do-it-yourself projects can give a girl that Bad Bridesmaid feeling, even if it's obvious the bride is simply trying to save money or add a personal touch to her nuptials.

No sooner had Jasmine P. been selected as one of five bridesmaids in a college friend's wedding than she began receiving weekly e-mails containing The Bride's "expecta-tions" for their "services" over the months to come. The group was referred to as The Bride's "ambassadors" and they were expected to reflect that title with every ounce of their will and every penny in their wallets.

One e-mail was a six-page list of jobs The Bride needed done before, during, and after the wedding, such as taking her dress to the cleaner's after the ceremony and address-ing her thank-you notes while she honeymooned. Subse-quent e-mails contained a briefing about "the image" of the wedding, and noted that every detail—along with the bridesmaid who did or did not make it happen—would send a clear message to the guests as to the event's success. The vein throbbing in The Bride's forehead would not dis-tract her assembled loved ones, she seemed to believe, but the wedding would be ruined if the seating plan was not immediately spell-checked.

Jasmine said she felt like she was being tested to see how far she would go in the name of friendship and to prove herself worthy of the wedding walk, like a reality show contestant eating pig testicles to earn one more minute of screen time or a shot at dating Flavor Flav.

The Bride would call Jasmine and her cohorts and instruct them to drop everything and rush to help her register, or demand they cancel their weekend plans at the last minute to look over her engagement photos—issuing a stream of orders that were as unrelenting as they were unreasonable.

"In any other situation, there's no way," said Jasmine. "But suddenly she has license because she's getting married."

Cassidy B. was asked to fill in for a bridesmaid who'd had the nerve to get pregnant during the engagement period and could not fulfill her duties, creating the need for a bridesmaid ringer. The Bride was a cousin by marriage, and Cassidy hardly knew her, but she still wound up taking orders from various members of The Bride's family, including her domineering mother.

"She gave me a list," the three-time bridesmaid said. "Go out and get this shower invitation, and this is what the invitation should say. Go and order these chairs from this person. Pick them up here and take them over there."

For four months, Cassidy obeyed commands, couriered furniture and family, and generally acted as a go-between and gofer, financing her tasks personally and cursing her bad luck.

"I spent about seven hundred dollars just doing errands," she said.

And as Martha might say, that's not a good thing.

DISAPPEARING SISTER ACT

Spending the early months of wedding prep attached at the hip to your former friend turned professional bride is tricky enough, but taking orders from your own flesh and blood can be doubly hard to bear. When Holly J. was a bridesmaid in her early twenties—in the years before e-mail (BE 1995)—she received a letter from her sister The Bride a week before the wedding, expressing disappointment that Holly had not been more helpful in the months that had passed since the engagement.

Holly was still in her last year of college, a virgin attendant who had not yet developed a keen interest in garter belts or garden parties, but even so she had been named the Maid of Honor, a role that puts the "horrific" in *honorific*. Today the MOH is the bride's second-in-command, and as such is expected to be only slightly less obsessed with the wedding than if it were her own. To put the icing on the proverbial wedding cake, Holly's sister is a hyper-organized Type-A personality, who had a two-year engagement and a penchant for color-coding each task.

"It was just spreadsheet after spreadsheet," Holly said. "We got maybe three a week, and there were constant updates."

As MOH, she had been assigned the color code blue, and her duties were highlighted accordingly; those of the best man in orange, and so on. Unfortunately, being in receipt of three dozen PowerPoint presentations did not fundamentally alter Holly's brain chemistry such that she was actually *willing* to execute all of her Code Blue ball-breaking duties. The Bride wanted a series of showers: a "Jack and Jill" party, where friends of both the bride and groom would gather to contribute money to the wedding; an engagement party; and a bachelorette. Holly did not know the protocol for any of these events, nor did she have the cash to finance them. Her sister also wanted the same people invited to each party, a gift-giving bonanza Holly was unwilling to inflict on friends or strangers.

The peculiar lunacy of brides is much like that of sheltered big-name celebrities—everyone knows they're bonkers, but no one is supposed to point it out. "Yes, you look much thinner in that, Ms. Alley." "Of course you should get another round of Botox, Ms. Kidman." "I think you two are perfect for each other, Miss Holmes." The built-in sympathy of siblings explains why so many movie stars hire their sisters as publicists: a family member is much less likely to max out on your madness or out you to the tabloids.

But Holly was not prepared to take orders from anyone, especially her big sis. "I said, 'No, I'm not going to throw you another shower,'" she recounted. "'You've already had five, and that's enough.'"

Speaking the words *that's enough* into the ear of a bride is much like blowing a high-pitched dog whistle in a room full of senior citizens—it just doesn't register. The letter The Bride sent Holly the week before the wedding made no reference to her own over-the-top expectations, but said that she and her fiancé were very disappointed that Holly hadn't done more to accommodate them and that she was being punished accordingly.

"They said, 'We don't want you to be a part of our day, and we feel it's best that you just attend the wedding and not be a part of the wedding party,'" Holly remembered. "If they had ripped out my heart and stomped on it, I wouldn't have felt as bad as I did when I read this thing."

Fortunately for Holly, the two women reconciled before the wedding day, and now that she is getting married herself, she claims to have found a new appreciation for the MOH role. Let's just say her sister's color-coded spreadsheets are looking pretty handy right about now.

Elaine W., on the other hand, said she was thrilled from the start to have been asked to stand up in her younger sister Melanie's wedding. Elaine was a three-timer and a self-professed lover of all things wedding, but toward the end of the yearlong engagement period, the two women were barely on speaking terms.

It began innocently enough, with shopping trips to find the dress and phone calls for advice on everything from flowers to ribbon and how to design the place cards. And then Elaine's boyfriend, Chris, volunteered to get into the mix, designing and producing the couple's wedding invitations. It was then that family relations began to unravel.

Though Chris worked diligently in the evenings and over weekends, it wasn't enough to sate the eager Bride. She'd originally said she needed the invites by early July, to mail out for the late-September wedding, yet by the beginning of June she was already harassing her sister about why they weren't finished.

"They were saving tons of cash, because if they had bought these it would have cost a thousand dollars at least," Elaine said. "But she started being rude to him over e-mail."

At the end of June, Melanie came to Elaine's apartment for a day of wedding-related shopping. She was an hour early, and her sister was not ready; her hair was a mess and she was still wearing her pajamas. "She looks at me and says 'nice hair,' and basically lectures me for being late," Elaine said, having missed the all-important "Shopping Begins an Hour Earlier than Scheduled" chapter in *Being a Bridesmaid for Dummies.*

When The Bride moved on from her sister and started pestering Chris about the invitations, Elaine could take it no more.

"I just freaked. I looked at her and said, 'You are so unappreciative. You're a goddamn bridezilla,'" she remembered. "Now that's obviously the biggest insult you can give a woman getting married. And the look on her face was pure hurt."

Elaine felt awful about what she had said, and called her sister into her bedroom to apologize. Before she could say I'm sorry and admit she should have been more sympathetic to her sister's stress, Melanie started screaming and flinging her Maid of Honor around by the arm. The women fought like professional wrestlers and trash-talked each other with vocabulary usually reserved for Tourette's patients. Eventually, the beleaguered Chris had to come in and separate them.

"I just became mean because of her," Elaine said, still obviously confused about the spell that came over her and her sister, who had also turned over an uncharacteristically freaky new leaf. "After that, I said she could call me if she needed something, but I'm not calling her."

All was not forgiven, and when her invitation came, the envelope was addressed to "Ms Elaine Wilson and Guest"—conspicuously devoid of her boyfriend's name.

"First of all, we've been dating for four years," Elaine said. "Second of all, he designed your fucking invitations!"

THERE'S NO *I* IN *SWEATSHOP*

Wedding planning today is about more than passive-aggressive decision making and bottled-up rage—it requires the nimble fingers of a Keebler elf and the creativity of a Bush administration spin doctor.

In the lead-up to two different weddings in which she served as a bridesmaid, Rita S. found herself enrolled in a bridal craft boot camp, required to channel her creative energy into strictly supervised artistic assignments. One bride, a friend she'd met in France during a high school exchange program, was an artist who wanted to customize her wedding by sending guests home with a handcrafted memento of her talents as a painter. Unfortunately, it was not actually her hands that would craft said keepsakes. More than 150 paperweight-size rocks were collected for the bridesmaids to paint with each guest's name and a design of The Bride's creation.

"They all had to be different—every single one," Rita said.

In the week leading up to the wedding, the bridesmaids were corralled into The Bride's backyard and outfitted with a pile of rocks and a small paintbrush. Each was given a list of names and specific instructions for design and color palettes. For hours on end, the women worked without so much as a cocktail to get their creative juices flowing. The sun beat down on their outdoor workshop as they bent over heaps of stones that grew hot in their hands, the paint running off into their laps, leaving lurid stains.

"Ninety-five-degree heat in her backyard with a little paintbrush," Rita said ruefully. "There was liquor at the wedding but not at the rock painting, which was clearly when we needed it."

After customizing a sackful of souvenir stones, Rita thought she had completed the most painstaking activity she would face as a bridesmaid. The next summer, however, in service to yet another bride, she found herself bent over an equally grueling task—this time involving the dexterous creation of bows and knots.

The Bride had chosen to save money by creating her own wedding invitations, and asked her bridesmaids over to help. Each invitation had two separate layers, and the sheets of delicate paper were to be tied together with thin silky ribbons. The Bride wanted each invite tied in an identical manner (naturally), with the ribbon strung through punched holes, twisted and turned, and then tied with a decorative flourish.

"I was terrible at it," said Rita. "It was incredibly torturous because we're sitting there in this, like, sweatshop with pieces of ribbon everywhere. And it was billed as a fun night. 'Come over for pizza and help me tie my invitations!'"

It took six women five hours to complete the job, and to this day Rita can't look at a wedding invitation without a pang of sympathy for the poor people in the Hallmark factory.

FORCED LABOR OF LOVE

Most bridesmaids will find themselves faced with at least one ridiculous, random, or tiresome task before their friend's wedding. When Yvonne S., a Toronto-based creative director, was asked to be a bridesmaid for the third time, she suddenly found herself single-handedly responsible for the aesthetic vibe of her friend's entire wedding. In her day job, Yvonne oversees the interior design of restaurants and nightclubs, and creates the backdrops for award shows and other large-scale media events. The Bride (and her mother) believed that such creative talent should not go unexploited in their own wedding extravaganza, and they elected

Yvonne as their BITCH (Bridesmaid In Total Ceremonial Hell). She was expected not only to create the wedding invitations but also to arrange the flowers and decorate the event space, accompanied by a crew of helpers conscripted into service like child soldiers in Sierra Leone, armed with glue guns instead of Kalashnikovs.

Thus, Yvonne's "bridesmaid" tasks spanned literally the entire engagement period and encompassed every possible permutation of research, planning, decision making, arts and crafts, and other minor atrocities endured by the lucky ladies in this chapter.

"E-mails, books, meetings, dinners—I was out with them a million times," she said. "Phone calls for days. It was crazy."

At one point early on in the planning, the Mother of the Bride summoned Yvonne to a meeting to show her sixteen amber vases she had bought at Costco, having made an executive decision before actually asking Yvonne: "Can we work with this?"

The glass cylinders were the centerpiece of the whole show, and the MOB wanted Yvonne to construct a theme, color scheme, and flower installation centered around their presence. The bridesmaid had no idea how she would build a wedding around maple syrup–colored containers, no matter how "exquisite" they were said to be.

"I felt like she was going to bite my head off if I said it wasn't okay, so I just went with 'yes,'" Yvonne said.

For the next few months, she searched high and low to find amber-hued ribbon to use as a runner on the tables at the reception. Eventually she gave up and settled on a pure white theme, with the amber vase anchors as a splash of color. This was not the end of her creative challenges. The family of The Bride regularly entertained in their home, and at one point, they invited Yvonne over and ushered her into the basement, where she found stacks of leftover dried flower arrangements, more vases, and seasonal décor.

"They said, 'You can use this, can't you?'" she aped.

The creative director suddenly found herself charged with incorporating into a summer wedding millions of silver twigs with fake berries—the stuff of sitcom Christmas specials and Pottery Barn clearance sales. She picked through the family's vase collection, discarding anything too brightly colored, ornate, better suited to an old folks' home, or seemingly once used as a bong by The Bride's younger brother.

The flowers themselves were another problem. Yvonne's arrangements were completely white, except for a single blue hydrangea in each one, meant to pick up on the blue tuxedo shirts the groomsmen had selected to add a dash of hipster irony to their attire. When Yvonne went to the reception hall for one last check on her creation, the blue blooms had already wilted in the summer heat, limp brown smudges in the otherwise pristine white room. Decked out in her bridesmaid dress, Yvonne ran around the event hall pulling hydrangeas from each bouquet like a deranged florist, doing her best not to destroy their arrangement or draw too much attention to her actions.

"I was trying to do it in a somewhat discreet way," she said. "Crushing them up as small as I could in my hands so no one would see what I was doing and be like, 'Why is she stealing the flowers out of the arrangements before the ceremony?'"

Unfortunately, it's tough to be discreet in head-to-toe tulle.

Most bridesmaids do their best to obey the commands of their Bridal Leader and accommodate last-minute disasters involving flowers or fashion, while silently counting down the days until it will all be over. Still, listening to nonstop wedding talk for a year of your life can take its toll on even the most dedicated bridesmaid.

This was sort of how I was feeling when I saw a tank top for sale on Going Bridal (www.goingbridal.com), a Web site that pokes fun at the over-the-top demands of modern brides. I thought it was hilarious and adequately apropos of the last few months of my life. The site sells cards that read "Thank you for the completely inadequate wedding present" and Greedy Bride T-shirts that show a woman in an elaborate gown and veil clutching a large wad of cash in one manicured fist. The shirt I picked out was white, with a photo of a bride framed by a red circle and slashed through with a single diagonal line. Beneath the image are the words, PLEASE SHUT UP ABOUT YOUR FUCKING WEDDING.

When my article about being a Bad Bridesmaid was published, it ran with a close-up photograph of my chest clad in the shirt, with a bouquet of flowers in my hands strategically arranged so that a single petal blocked the obscene word from view.

I have since realized that donning such a garment around a prospective bride is a form of bridesmaid hara-kiri, like wearing a shirt that says, "That makes your ass look big" while working retail, or busting out your "I like little boys" tee on a Cub Scout retreat. It just won't go over well.

The founder of Going Bridal is not the only person who has been inspired to create a 100-percent-cotton protest to pre-wedding obligations. Olivia T. was thirty years old when a woman she had known since childhood asked her to be in her wedding party. They'd met when they were eight and had been close growing up, but twenty-two years later they saw each other only about once a year. Soon after her friend's engagement, though, Olivia and five other bridesmaids were meeting on a monthly basis to discuss every element of the wedding, shop for dresses, and receive updates on the *Farmers' Almanac*–projected weather forecast for the wedding day.

For more than a year, Olivia attended parties once a month, arriving at each with a strictly assigned gift: for the lingerie shower ($50), the Home Depot shower ($75), and even a wine shower ($40), where the guests dozed while the engaged couple read out the name of each bottle, the year it was produced, and who it was from.

"It was like: 'Masi, 1999, Mike and Kathy Smith; Penfolds Estate, 2001, Debby and Matthew Reynolds; Twin Fin, 2006, Hank and Betty Jackson,'" Olivia said. "And then they'd grab the next bottle of wine. It was brutal."

In between the regularly scheduled events, the bridesmaids also had to meet to go over flower arrangements, bouquets, finger foods, and who would officiate the ceremony. For an unknown reason, these details could not be discussed via e-mail or on the phone—which would at least have allowed the bridesmaids to roll their eyes or watch TV while being gradually bored to death. No, this bride wanted her planning intimate and interactive. At one meeting, the women gathered for a two-hour powwow over whether the necklines on their bridesmaid dresses should sit just below the collarbone or just above. Each bridesmaid had to take turns sharing her opinion as The Bride took notes, and the relative merits of conservatism and décolletage were discussed.

"I remember thinking it was the stupidest conversation I'd ever been a part of in my whole life," Olivia said.

By the time the engagement period was over, she and the other bridesmaids had spent thousands of dollars on gifts, lunches, lattes, and decorations, and most of them had given up entirely on being helpful or cooperative. They were sick of The Bride, the groom, and of each other, having spent more time boring one another to tears than the cast of *Everybody Loves Raymond*.

At the wedding reception, Olivia said the bridesmaids were itching for escape, eager to be finished with the year-long endeavor. Little did they know that they would soon have a lasting memento of their 365-day sacrifice. In front of three hundred wedding guests at the formal black-tie function, a groomsman took the microphone and made a toast to the bridesmaids. He paid tribute to how well they had all gotten to know one another, a product, he noted, of twelve months of forced get-togethers and mandated social interaction. And to illustrate his point, he presented each bridesmaid with a T-shirt that read I SURVIVED THE LINDA-STEVE WEDDING TOUR.

The T-shirts were modeled after the concert tees sold at every live rock show from the Rolling Stones to the Pussy-cat Dolls. On the front, photos of the bride and groom grinned out at the guests like deranged teen idols, and on the back were listed the dates, venues, and themes of every wedding-related meeting, shower, and engagement bash the bridesmaids had been forced to attend.

Across the rundown of events were stamped the words SOLD OUT in bright red letters. The neckline sat just above the collarbone, as discussed.

3

SEA FOAM BLUES

It's a bridesmaid's dress. Someone loved it intensely for one day. Then, tossed it . . . like a Christmas tree. So special, then bam—it's on the side of the road, tinsel still clinging to it, like a sex crime victim, underwear inside out, bound with electrical tape.

—MARLA SINGER, *Fight Club*

I didn't want to come out of the dressing room.

It was springtime and we were shopping for the brides-maid dresses that I and three other girls would wear down the aisle in July. The outing had started out like any other weekend shopping trip with friends. It was a gorgeous, brisk but sunny Saturday morning and The Bride, another bridesmaid, and I strolled through a trendy shopping dis-trict laughing at people's outfits and chatting about where we would stop for lunch. The sidewalks were crammed with street vendors, hot dog salesmen, and women jump-ing the gun on summer, barelegged under their flirty skirts, despite the chilly breeze. Music blared from outdoor speakers and we ducked in and out of stores if something pretty caught our eye. We were not, however, the only female shoppers on the strip, and our bubble of bridal bliss would soon be burst. As we were planning our best friend's wedding, the city was abuzz with a different sort of major event planning. It was high school prom time, and the malls were teeming with teenage Lolitas, strutting around in size-zero jeans and taunting us with their tiny frames.

Psychologically, I wasn't ready to hunt for dresses along-side three hundred ninety-pound debutantes. I didn't want to hear them talk about how their minuscule asses looked fat or be forced to contemplate how many years had gone by since my own high school graduation, when I regret-tably wore a dress I had made myself and hemmed with purple feathers.

Physically, I was equally unprepared for the task at hand. It was still cool enough outside to require socks, and I had wisely selected a dark pair that were sure to look fantastic when worn with my Hush Puppies and a strap-less peach cocktail dress. It should also be noted that underwear has never been my thing, and I had convinced myself that going commando while dress shopping was an acceptable way to avoid having my pantyline pointed out by a stick-thin saleswoman who probably ironed her thong before putting it on. And so I found myself clad in a cheap, off-white gauzy number that I had managed to zip up over my pasty white back, my private areas fully visible through the translucent material, my socks and shoes doing little to heighten the outfit's already minimal appeal, wondering how I could avoid showing it to my friends.

The small curtained dressing room stall in which I stood did not even provide me with a mirror, let alone a window through which to escape, so I emerged with only a vague idea of the disaster that awaited me. Outside, I was con-fronted by my startlingly unglamorous reflection in the full-length mirror, the store's fluorescent lights making matters worse with their sickly strobe-light flickering. It would have been less painful for everyone involved had I just walked out buck naked. At least then I might have gotten a laugh.

As I had feared, the sheets of gauzy taffeta were not successful in creating an opaque layer, and the dress was as transparent as the look of disgust on the faces of my fellow shoppers. My body, in all its post-winter, pre-diet glory, was hidden by only a fine mist of poorly constructed fabric and the length of my two black tube socks. Across the store, a sixteen-year-old emerged from another dressing room wearing the exact same dress, with a pink slip under-neath and high heels on her pedicured feet, her perfectly toned frame a cruel reminder of how my own body had looked before I was introduced to beer, Beaujolais, and brie. She was my polar opposite reflected back at me. And I swear I saw her smirk.

PUTTING UP A STINK

How a woman looks in a bridesmaid dress can sometimes be secondary to how it makes her feel. Wedding attendants are asked to cheerfully contend with cheap material, unforgiving seams, and boning that threatens to puncture a lung if you exhale too deeply or turn sharply to your right.

Aynsley F., an eight-timer, was made to wear a formal suit constructed from fabric she suspected had been torn from a couch. "It was one of the ugliest dresses I'd ever seen in my life," she said. "It was taffeta but it looked like upholstery. It was a mauve skirt and a jacket and there was a ruffle over the butt."

To make matters worse, she was participating in an August wedding that took place in an old, unairconditioned church in the heart of the Deep South. "It was a long Catholic wedding in Spanish and English—twice as long because they had to do it in both languages," Aynsley remembered.

The bridesmaids wore shoes that were so cheap they began to disintegrate at the first sign of sweat. By the end of the service, they'd each lost a dress size in perspiration, their Tammy Bakker mascara streaming down their cheeks, the ruffles on their butts sagging with the weight of absorbed water, and their former kitten heels compressed into flats. They had been reduced to a lineup of deflated, soaking-wet women who looked as though they had just worked an eight-hour secretarial shift inside a sauna.

It must be awful to stand through a summer wedding draped in the skin of an old couch, but imagine what it would be like to attend a wedding in a bridesmaid dress that has *already* been worn and drenched in sweat.

Twenty-eight-year-old Erica P. was in a wedding where the bridesmaids' dresses were hand-me-downs from the nuptials of one of The Bride's relatives. "The dress I had to wear had been previously worn by someone with the most horrific body odor," said the three-time attendant. The Bride promised she would have the dress dry-cleaned and told Erica not to worry, the only scents permeating her wedding day would be those of fresh flowers and her own desperation to finally tie the knot.

When the dress came back, Erica pulled it out of the plastic bag and got a noseful of BO. "It was too strong for even the cleaners to get out!" she said. Throughout the wedding, the bridesmaid trailed a cloud of stink around with her dress—down the aisle and back, into the reception, and even during the group and family photos, when she had to sit on the knee of one of the groomsmen, the armpit of her dress dangerously close to his nose.

"I had to apologize for the smell of this dress I'm wearing," she said. "And of course, how many of them do you think believed that the dress smelled BEFORE I put it on?"

PRETTY AWFUL IN PINK

A few women may have to wear secondhand bridesmaid dresses, but it is a rule of modern society that no one ever wears a bridesmaid dress twice, no matter how many times they are assured of its timelessness, comfort, and durability.

Every bride tries to convince her bridesmaids that their dresses will be stunning couture worthy of a future red carpet or black-tie ball. Because of this lie, women who swear by designer labels, fashion-forward thinking, and black, black, black suddenly find themselves decked out in cheap knockoff strapless numbers in a shade of putrid purple. Almost every woman has one of these dresses in her closet, tucked away in the section reserved for things that are never worn but were too expensive to throw out, like that designer poncho that seemed like such a good idea or the three-hundred-dollar skinny jeans that you were too fat to wear after a four-dollar McDonald's meal. And when it comes to their bridesmaid dresses—like a lot of painful experiences masquerading as important milestones—women tend to remember their first time.

"The Bride first let us know that she wanted us in pink by sending an e-mail," said Madeline J., by now a five-time bridesmaid. This kind of message is among the scariest things that can happen to a woman via computer, second only to the terrifying moment when you accidentally click on a pop-up window at work and find your monitor filled with multiplying images of hard-core pornography. Rather than let The Bride's demand spiral similarly out of control, Madeline and her fellow bridesmaids wrote her back, each crafting carefully worded responses that said they supported her decision but implied that they were worried about its color-coordinated consequences.

"Well, it's your wedding, but be aware that because of my skin tone, many shades of pink make me look like I'm not wearing anything," Madeline wrote in her own reply. "Not that I mind that particularly, but it is after all *your* day and the attention should be focused on you."

Psychological double-talk of this manner is the only acceptable weapon against a butt-ugly bridesmaid dress. Brides are known to respond to unfiltered opinion as if you've asked them to let the groom's ex-girlfriend jump out of a cake at his bachelor party. Words such as *hideously ugly* must be replaced with *potentially inappropriate*, and the term "I'd rather die than put that on my body" substituted with "Don't you think it might clash with your flowers?" This sort of dubious dishonesty is not usually perfected until the later stages of motherhood, when women must convince their children that they are being punished for their own good.

As it happened, this bride stuck by her choice, secure in the knowledge that it did not even come close to the color of a pale girl's skin. Madeline should have been so lucky.

"It was *so* pink. It was not even fuchsia. Not pale pink. It was fluorescent highlighter pink," she said, still awed by the dress's nuclear capabilities years after she wore it. "It was its own light source." The dress was also floor length, A-line, shiny satin, and multiplied six times, making the brides-maids look like Dolly Parton's backup singers, circa 1982.

Just when you thought it couldn't get any more humili-ating for these poor pink bridal attendants, Madeline delivered the kicker: "She made us skip into the wedding reception."

More than a wearable wedding accessory, the bridesmaid dress has developed into a modern tool of female ritual humiliation. One suspects that there is a global conspiracy afoot to persuade women to dress up like idiots and bound down an aisle—a way to turn us against each other so we can never unite toward the goal of total world domination.

Sometimes technology has a hand in this process, complicating—or completely crashing—a wedding pro-gram already fraught with peril. Two-time bridesmaid Grace L. was in a wedding where The Bride ordered her attendants' dresses from an Internet boutique. Most bridal parties will consider this option, clicking through page after page of calf-length strapless gowns modeled by girls who would never actually be caught dead in them in public. Online, a lot of outfits look nice, but then again, a lot of people who post dating profiles on the Internet seem normal until you get back to their apartment and find a collection of rubber bondage masks hanging on the mantel. The dress Grace and her fellow bridesmaids were to wear looked pretty good on the computer screen, a strapless, empire-waisted gown in a bold color that was just modern enough without being gaudy.

"It was hot pink, which I thought could have been pretty cool," Grace said.

When the dresses were delivered, the women realized that they'd been duped, as if their Russian mail order bride had turned up and told them she was only in it for the green card.

The outfits were as badly constructed as Scott Peterson's alibi, the seams framing every inch of their tummies and highlighting all their fleshy flaws. The top was not boned, so it hung dangerously loose, threatening to collapse at the faintest provocation. And instead of being one hot pink dress, the outfit was constructed from two layers of fabric: a white sliplike foundation topped by a see-through organza overlay in bright, blinding fuchsia. Like an out-of-control science project, the fusion of the two materials created a color that was not so much hot pink as discarded Bubblicious.

"We looked like wads of gum," Grace sighed.

BROWN BUNNIES AND
SHRIMPY EIGHTIES PROM QUEENS

Until the nineteenth century, it would have been unheard of for a bridesmaid to wear pink—bubble gum or otherwise. Before then, bridal attendants were dressed head to toe in white, designed as clones of the bride, to distract evil spirits or jealous ex-suitors.

When the threat of wedding-day abductions and evil curses subsided in the Western world, brides were no longer content to let their friends steal their thunder by wearing outfits similar to their own. White was phased out to satisfy brides' growing desire to be the center of attention, and bridesmaids were dressed instead in coordinated hues of pale blue, pink, lilac, or green, like a collection of animated Easter M&Ms.

Forgetting that the bridal attendant role had been created to save their pretty little asses from being kidnapped or cursed, brides soon started making other additions to ensure that their bridesmaids looked nowhere near as good as they did, beginning a trend that has lasted to this day.

If you think you've got it bad, consider the poor bridesmaids of 150 years ago, who had to wear bonnets, or the women photographed in Jules Schwerin's book *Wedding Styles: The Ultimate Bride's Companion*, who are clutching "fashionable shepherd's crooks" in their white-knuckled hands. The motive for this Little Bo Peep theme, one has to assume, was to make the dowdy bride look like an absolute fox by comparison.

Considering that our historical foremothers were dressed like formal shepherds, modern bridesmaids have little to complain about in the form of tiered skirts, sweetheart necklines, plunging backs, or high collars, but there is still something about bridesmaid dresses for everyone to hate.

"It was the tackiest red I'd ever seen in my life," Sally N. said of the dress chosen for her friend's wedding, a satin number with flounces. "It wasn't like a really pretty deep red or any sort of classic red. It was Mexican whore red.

And no offense to whores in Mexico, but it looked like it belonged in a bordello."

Another bridesmaid wore a dress that was described to her as the color of shrimp. "I imagined shit-filled veins and spindly legs," said Pamela B. The dress was also so loose that when she first tried it on she could see straight down through the neckline and to her feet. Ninety dollars in alterations later, the pale pink material had been cinched around her frame, and Pamela said she felt like an eighties prom queen: "A shrimpy eighties prom queen."

Bridesmaids who once admired the bride's ability to re-create the pages of *Vogue* in her own daily wardrobe may be surprised when she instructs them to dress as extras in Stephen King's *Carrie* or dancers in an ABBA reunion concert. But sadly, no number of bad reviews or desperate pleas from a bridesmaid are enough to shake loose the bride's grip on her chosen gown.

When Kate F., a thirty-one-year-old mother of two, was selected as a bridesmaid for her childhood friend, she told The Bride that the dress she had chosen was unflattering at best. "She didn't seem to really care that none of us were going to look good," said Kate. "She gracefully offered to pay for half of it, which was very kind. But she wanted us to have it that badly."

The dress in question also had an empire waist and flowed out from the bustline into a train at the back. From the chest down it was entirely formless, except for the puckering from the badly sewn seams, which created a rippled effect down the bridesmaids' sides. "My step-mother-in-law, who's a judge, was speechless," Kate said. "How hard is it to leave a judge speechless?" Adding to her distress, the dress was deep brown with a blue bow for trim. "At first I thought it made me look like a chocolate Easter bunny. But I didn't even look that good."

Sometimes, shopping for a bridesmaid dress provides the first indication that two women who have felt so close in every other aspect of their lives have diametrically opposed ideas about style. One woman's dream dress can be another's knee-length nightmare with spaghetti straps.

A few weeks after being named to a bridal party, successful fashion buyer Hilary M. received a phone call from her friend The Bride telling her the dresses had been found, and all she had to do was traipse on over to the store and pick hers up. As soon as she crossed over the threshold of the down-market clothing chain, Hilary knew she was in trouble.

"Already I was panicking," she said. "I looked at everything in the store and just knew I would never wear any of it."

Her own sporty-chic aesthetic was nowhere to be found among the racks of oh-so-over peasant blouses and shelves of bright pink shrugs. When she got to the counter, the saleswoman smiled supportively and handed her a two-piece dress constructed from iridescent green-blue taffeta, with a teeny-tiny tank and a full, billowy skirt.

"The top is basically just a square of fabric at the front with a tie across the back," Hilary said, shuddering at the memory. "It's backless, so you can't wear a bra. And anyone who knew me would know that they could not send me down an aisle without a bra."

She started to cry as soon as the aqua monstrosity hit her body, and dialed The Bride from her cell phone inside the dressing room while trying to hold the outfit over her double-D boobs with her free hand.

"I don't think I can wear this," she stammered through her tears, staring at her Little-Mermaid-turns-tricks reflection. Instead of asking her friend if she had lost her mind, or inquiring if the wedding was being filmed for an episode of *Playboy*'s *Bridesmaids Gone Wild: Vegas Style*, Hilary grasped for the first logical excuse to reject the dress that crossed her mind.

The tattoo on her back would be visible in such a revealing gown, she reasoned, and guests might find it inappropriate. It should have been a foolproof rationale—visible tattoos are up there on most women's lists of Wedding Don'ts, along with chili dog appetizers and Guns N' Roses cover bands. Hilary had no idea what levels of inappropriateness The Bride could handle, but she was about to find out.

"She said, 'That's okay, we'll just cover it up with those stick-on jewel things,'" Hilary said, her voice still filled with disbelief. "That's where I drew the line. I'll walk down the aisle with my tits at my belly button, but you're not gluing any glitter to my back."

PROJECT RUN AWAY

Ready-to-wear gowns that don't stink—literally or figuratively—can be hard to find for any individual, let alone for groups of women whose bodies are as different as their income levels and natural hair colors. So instead of searching for matching dresses they can buy off the rack, many bridal parties find themselves perusing pattern books to select their gowns. And in the hopes of tailoring a design to suit their own figures, they will subject themselves to the grizzled gaze and surprisingly strong grip of dressmakers who wrap tape measures around their bodies like tourniquets and produce, several months later, a loose approximation of the dress they had in mind.

When Suzy F. and her fellow bridesmaids went for their fittings, the seamstress would break out the pins and start jabbing them with verbal abuse of her own design.

"The dresses look better on the skinny girls," she said to one.

"Did you know your hips are not symmetrical?" she told another. "You should avoid low-rise pants."

"Good thing the shawl will cover up those broad shoulders," she remarked to the third.

At her last appointment, Suzy found that her dress was cut just a little snug. The seamstress sighed before conceding that she could let the garment out at the sides, a concept she presented like an act of martyrdom. Made to feel personally responsible for the dress's lung-restricting dimensions, the bridesmaid took a deep breath and promised to lose weight. The dressmaker did not discourage her from fasting or apologize for making the dress one size too small, she simply nodded and barked, "Three to five pounds should do it."

With the bridesmaid's fate and cash deposit in her calloused, dye-stained hands, the dressmaker can say anything she wants, but pity the woman who insults the dress—or the needlework—in return.

Kirsty J. remembers arriving to be fitted for the dress she affectionately refers to as The Pink Sausage. "It had spaghetti straps like when you were a teenager and it was long and had slits up either side that basically went all the way up," she said. "I'm not Catholic, but I did not feel comfortable walking through a church in this thing."

While Kirsty managed to keep her dismay to herself, her best friend, a bridesmaid in the same wedding, let her true feelings slip. She had gone in for a fitting by herself and was soon on the receiving end of the seamstress's dissertation on the magic of marriage. On and on the woman talked as Kirsty's friend was being pinned into her dress, asking if she was excited and if she agreed that weddings were, like, the most romantic things ever.

Finally, the bridesmaid could take it no more.

"She said, 'You know, weddings aren't really everybody's idea of the ultimate fantasy, and I actually can't believe I have to walk down the aisle in this thing,'" Kirsty recounted. The occupants of the bridal boutique froze as if the curtain had finally dropped, the Wizard of Gauze visible for all to see, cranking up the hype on his fragile matrimonial kingdom. "Everyone turned around and just glared at her," Kirsty said. "She ran back into the dressing room and called me to come down and save her."

Having a bridesmaid dress custom-made is not necessarily torturous for every bridal party. It may be the sole opportunity for women to insert their own personality and flair, turning the dress-selection process into a competitive sport, an opportunity to outdo one another and even (uh-oh) the bride.

Why add to your wardrobe a boring dress you'll never wear again when you can add an outrageous, backless, bias-cut dress you'll never wear again?

Jenny T. was in a wedding where each of the fourteen bridesmaids was given four yards of green fabric and told to design her own dress along with the help of a seamstress of her choice. "It was a competition," she said. "It was unbelievable."

The Bride's rules stated that the dress had to be floor-length and use the shiniest side of the material, which was a glowing shade of seaweed no matter which way you turned it. The friends had attended a wedding the year before with a similar design edict, and one bridesmaid had reversed the fabric, producing a dress a shade lighter than everyone else's. "She wanted to be different," Jenny said. "Can you imagine? It just looked so stupid."

Jenny selected a pattern for a fitted dress with wide straps that sat just off the shoulder and dropped her fabric and design off with a reasonably priced dressmaker, whose name she had found in the phone book. Three of the other bridesmaids, meanwhile, took the opportunity to create the dresses of their dreams. They hired designers who charged them a thousand dollars each to create custom-made gowns, with the women sketching out their fantasies and demanding their own little slice of haute couture. On the day of the wedding, the bridesmaids gathered for the "big reveal," anxious to see who had created the ultimate in underling fashion.

Some had their dresses intricately beaded and one girl's was ruched from top to bottom, a dramatic pillar of sweeping lines. Two were outfitted with halter tops, one had a boat neck, and eight were strapless A-line dresses.

When each girl walked in wearing her customized con-coction, the other women would scream and gush over how much they loved her dress. And when she went into the other room for a coffee or a pee, they would whisper to each other how hideous her outfit was and how much better they looked in their own.

"It was," Jenny said, "a total bitch fest."

DESPERATE MEASUREMENTS

Even if you don't hire Zac Posen to design your outfit, or have it customized with hand-glued Swarovski crystals, the average bridesmaid dress now costs between $200 and

$300—roughly the equivalent of a month's rent in a small town or a week's worth of groceries in the big city. And that's before the cost of alterations.

Martha C. received her dress three days before her college friend's wedding—and three months after it was ordered—at a cost of $225. The bridal party had selected their dresses (a top with buttons up the back paired with a long skirt) on the Internet, requesting three versions in three different sizes. The other two bridesmaids were five-foot-nine and extremely slender, ordering a size zero and a size two, respectively, and Martha is just shy of five feet and wears a size twelve.

When the order showed up on the manufacturer's end, the numbered sizes appeared as 0 2 1 2, and the company believed the group had accidentally ordered four dresses instead of three. Confused, an employee called The Bride's mother and asked how many dresses they wanted. When the MOB answered "three," they arbitrarily sent a zero and two size twos.

"So I had roughly forty-eight hours to figure out how to get my size twelve ass into that dress," Martha said.

In a panic, she searched frantically for fabric that was similar to the dress. She then went to a seamstress, who agreed to insert new panels, transforming a size two into a size twelve overnight. Unfortunately, the seamstress overcompensated a little in her rush to the finish line. When Martha got dressed on the day of the wedding, the ensemble was far too big. The buttons kept slipping out of the holes, and the back of her dress would open up to reveal that the skirt was pulled up to her chest.

"Every time the waitress would serve a course of the meal, she would put the plate down with one hand and do up my buttons with the other," said Martha. "The dress ended up costing me $430."

To avoid this last-minute expense, some women adopt a do-it-yourself attitude toward alterations. Allison P. was named Maid of Honor for her best friend when they were both still in college, and The Bride found inexpensive dresses for her wedding party so they wouldn't have to dip into their student loans to pay for them. The Bride had fallen in love with a lilac-colored dress with a simple boxy cut and straps that criss-crossed down the back, dotted with tiny rosettes. Allison did not hate the dress, but when she held it up to her body, she saw that it was cut for a woman half her height.

"It's made for a much shorter person," said the five-foot-ten and curvy bridesmaid. "The hem on me hit probably mid-calf."

The spaghetti straps and open back also meant that a bra was out of the question despite Allison's ample chest. The dress was bought against her reservations, and The Bride tried to comfort her buxom friend by telling her she could make any alterations she wanted, as long as the rosettes—and her breasts—remained firmly in place.

Allison set about turning the ill-fitting dress into something slightly less revealing but somehow even more absurd. "The dress came with this chiffon shawl wrap thing," she said. "So while everyone else had their wrap nicely draped over their arms, I basically took mine and built it into the dress." First, she bunched the shawl around the straps so her bra would be covered, then wove it through the criss-crossed panels between her shoulder blades to render the back of the dress opaque. "But [The Bride] didn't want me to cut the shawl, so there was this sort of tail hanging out of the bottom," Allison went on, "so I ended up with this chiffon criss-crossed braided mess at the back of the dress, a chiffon tail, and these cappy chiffon sleeves. It looked ridiculous."

Still, Allison probably didn't stick out as much as she thought. Consider the fate of another bridesmaid in the same wedding, who could not afford to alter a dress that was equally ill suited for her tiny frame. In the wedding photos, Allison's dress just barely scrapes her knees, her improvised straps creating billowing shoulder pads, while the other girl, a tiny thing, drowns inside a dress that is at least four sizes too big, the straps falling off her shoulders and two feet of extra material pooled at her feet.

Allison's design looked almost sophisticated by comparison.

MAIL-ORDER BRIDEZILLA

Bridesmaids may wear the dress down the aisle, but it is the garment that carries the ultimate power. Without their matching outfits, wedding attendants are nothing more than a bunch of pissed-off and pissed-drunk women who get to sit at the head table and see their names printed on the program.

Gemma H., a five-timer, had ordered her bridesmaid dress months in advance of her friend's wedding and well before the other six women who were acting as bridal attendants. The group had picked out their look online—further victims of an Internet shopping phenomenon that creates more confusion and regret than accidentally hitting Reply All after typing something dirty about your boss.

The gown was a pastel green two-piece with an A-line skirt and spaghetti straps, to be delivered to a store in The

Bride's hometown, about a forty-five-minute drive from where Gemma lived. Hers happened to arrive first, a month or so before the wedding, and The Bride offered to pick it up herself and give it to Gemma the next time they met.

The handoff, however, proved more difficult than they had anticipated. The two women would pick a day when they were both available, but The Bride would cancel at the last minute with a forgotten-appointment or emergency excuse.

"Every time I called her to go get it she ended up backing out," Gemma remembered. "And there were a couple of times when I made a real effort to get the dress."

There were now just three weeks until the wedding, and Gemma was scheduled to leave her East Coast home for a two-week vacation in California. When she got home, there would be only days until the wedding, and The Bride would be too busy to deliver the dress. Gemma offered two choices: The Bride could be available to hand it off on a specific date, or she could FedEx it to Gemma's home and the bridesmaid would absorb the cost. The Bride agreed to courier the dress, but instead of shelling out the ten dollars to send it overnight, she bundled it up and sent it regular mail. The package was headed just one town over, she reasoned, so she also waived insurance for her special delivery.

Unfortunately, when The Bride was addressing the package, she accidentally wrote the wrong zip code.

"The dress never arrived," Gemma said.

She returned from vacation, but the package had not turned up. Every day she would run to the mailbox, getting more and more worried that it wouldn't show up for the big day. The Bride began calling the postal service on a daily basis, begging them to find the dress and even offering a reward for information on its whereabouts.

One day, Gemma's husband asked the postman if he had seen a package with their names on it kicking around the mail room.

"He said, 'Oh gosh, are you guys the bridesmaid dress house?'" Gemma recalled. "She had everyone looking for it."

Five of the other bridesmaids had picked up their dresses by now, and the sixth, who lived in Seattle, had received hers in the mail two days after it was sent from the East Coast bride. Gemma held out hope until the last moment, thinking she could still get the outfit altered on the day of, if necessary, but ultimately resigned herself to the fact that if she had nothing to wear, she had no claim to be in the party.

"The day before, I said, 'Well, I guess I'm not in the wedding,' and [The Bride] said, 'No, I guess not,'" Gemma remembered.

The Bride felt bad about the mix-up, but Gemma said she was not as apologetic or upset as she could have been. "She said to me, 'If this is going to be the worst thing that's going to happen at my wedding, that's not so bad.' I was like, 'Oh, thanks.'"

After the wedding, Gemma kept checking the mail hoping that the wayward gown would arrive and she could donate it to charity, claiming the $150 price as a tax write-off. It never did.

"I truly believe that some twelfth-grader in Ohio wore my bridesmaid dress to her prom," she said.

BABY BUMPED

Tina M. was also expecting a delivery when she was asked to stand up as a bridesmaid for a lifelong friend. The twenty-four-year-old was newly married and ready for her first child. "I explained to her that I was trying to get pregnant and that the timing wouldn't be right as far as sizing the dress," she said.

The Bride assured Tina that it would be no problem, invoking her sister-in-law who had just been a bridesmaid while she was nine months pregnant. When the time came, Tina explained to the saleswoman that she needed to order a much larger size than would fit her current measurements.

Instead of saying congratulations and suggesting a good maternity bra to match the dress, the saleswoman did her best impersonation of the scene in *Pretty Woman* where Julia Roberts is expelled from a Rodeo Drive boutique. Store policy prevented women from ordering anything more than two sizes too big, the saleswoman explained haughtily, an arbitrary and nonsensical rule that she refused to bend for the sake of a baby.

"So I measured at a size ten and plunked down ninety dollars for a size twelve bridesmaid dress that was made of the unforgiving fabric of chiffon over satin," Tina said. "I remember thinking, 'I can't wait to see how this is going to turn out.'"

In June, Tina was five months pregnant and went for her last fitting at the bridal boutique. Her stomach was swollen with child, the elastic waistband on her pants as tight as the saleswoman's ass. She pulled the dress over her head, knowing deep down that the zipper would not close. The snobbish saleswoman stood there for several minutes, her hand on her chin, and for a moment Tina was convinced that she was going to tell her that she would have to lose the baby. In the end, the woman coldly and unapologetically informed her that there was nothing to be done, because they had built in only half an inch of extra material even though they had known she was pregnant.

"I had two more weeks of growth to go before the wedding," said Tina. "I stood there looking at the dress hanging on my bloated body, thinking, 'Oh, I'm so screwed.'"

The store said it was too late to order another dress, and Tina was forced to call The Bride and explain that she literally had nothing to wear. The Bride did not take the news well, nor did she take out her frustrations on the store and its size-ist attitude. "She told me that she'd had a list of the bridesmaids and ushers professionally printed that were to be placed on all the plates on the tables of the wedding guests," she said. "And now they couldn't be used, and that it was a waste of money."

Tina, of course, still had to pay for her dress.

PLAYING THE MASTER CARD

It's easy to blame Bad Bridesmaid experiences on dressmakers and store clerks, but just imagine the number of dysfunctional bridal parties they have had to deal with in their time. Deborah McCoy, a wedding planner who owns her own bridal store in Boca Raton, Florida, said she nearly stopped stocking bridesmaid dresses because of the drama it entailed, and changed the policy in her boutique to contend with imploding wedding parties.

Originally, when brides ordered their attendants' gowns, McCoy asked for a 50 percent deposit up front and the rest of the cost when the dresses came in. She discovered, though, that bridesmaids frequently went bye-bye before the dresses were even sewn, with a bride throwing her friend out of the wedding or the attendant storming off in disgust.

"I'd be stuck with the dresses," McCoy explained. "So I said, 'I want all of it up front.' That's how bad it got."

A bridesmaid dress designer named Sadie T. witnessed a *Surreal Life*-quality bridal party meltdown when a bride changed her mind about the gowns at the last minute. The woman had come in to the store weeks earlier with three of her five bridesmaids, and they had all happily settled on the idea of selecting individual styles in the same color and fabric.

"The girls were going to end up in a dress that they were comfortable in, in a color that they looked good in, and they were so excited," Sadie said.

She should have known it would never be that easy. On the day of the group's first consultation, The Bride swept in with all five bridesmaids in tow, and while they selected the style of their individual dresses, she was busy putting a kink in their plans. She sidled over to a rack of last season's styles and zeroed in on a strapless gold brocade number from the store's Fall/Winter collection that screamed of fabric-induced heatstroke. "It's beautiful, but the wedding is in the middle of August," Sadie said. "The dresses are made from heavy, heavy synthetic brocade and are lined in acetate. I don't care if it's strapless, you would die in that dress in the summer."

By that point, unfortunately, The Bride had abandoned reason along with the promise that her attendants would be comfortable. She pulled the dress off the rack and instructed one of the bridesmaids to try it on. To show that they were willing to be good sports, all of the women tried on the dress, hoping to demonstrate how bad it looked and how much each of them truly hated it. The gold hue did not complement anyone's coloring, and the conservative cut made them look like a woman's choir about to perform at an abstinence convention.

"A couple of them were kind of okay with the shape but none of them liked the fabric," Sadie said. "But the bride just made the executive decision, 'You're all going to wear this dress.'"

With those seven little words, the store descended into chaos. The girls asked The Bride why she had abandoned their original plan, begged her to reconsider, and even threw down a trump card when they felt they were cornered, pointing out that she would now have to change the color of their bouquets, which had already been ordered.

Unmoved, The Bride told them her decision was final, and that her bridesmaids would wear brocade. It was then that things turned ugly. The bridesmaids started screaming profanities at their friend as she yelled over and over, "It's my day! It's my day!" The wedding attendants called her selfish and The Bride told them if they were really her friends they would do as she said. Throughout it all, the Father of the Bride sat in a corner at the back of the store, smiling serenely. He did not intervene or offer an opinion, chastise his daughter, or apologize for the ruckus.

"He just crossed his hands, like, 'Whatever my baby wants, my baby gets,'" Sadie recalled with dismay.

With no chance of a third-party intervention, the bridal party broke off into groups to plan their next move. Two of the bridesmaids consoled The Bride, smoothing her hair and telling her that everything would work out fine. The other three gathered in a huddle at the front of the store, the defensive line planning their last, desperate Hail Mary pass. It was clear no one was going to back down and, like Paris Hilton and Nicole Richie, each would forever blame the other for the demise of their relationship.

Finally, the disgruntled bridesmaids asked The Bride flat out to make a decision between them and the dresses. Her response came without a pause: "If you were really my friends, you wouldn't make me choose."

"They said, 'Okay, that's all we need to hear. Find your-self three more fucking bridesmaids,'" Sadie remembered. "And they left. They stormed out."

By this point the other two bridesmaids were sobbing, The Bride was pale, and Sadie held her breath to see what would happen next. She expected The Bride to run after her friends or at least apologize to her for creating such a disturbance in the store. Instead, to everyone's surprise, The Bride reached into her purse.

"She took out her Visa," Sadie said, "slammed it down on the counter, paid for two gold brocade strapless dresses, and walked out."

Whatever baby wants, baby gets.

4

THE GOLDEN SHOWER

I did a little mental addition and over the years, I have bought Keira an engagement gift, a wedding gift—then there was the trip to Maine for the wedding—and three baby gifts. In total, I have spent over $2,300 celebrating *her* choices.

—CARRIE BRADSHAW, *Sex and the City*

The Bride wanted patio furniture.

This was the news that filtered through the bridal party in the early weeks of April, as we began planning the requisite shower for our friend's impending nuptials.

My own patio furniture came with the apartment I share with my boyfriend—an assortment of cheap white plastic covered in a film of grime, booze, grease from the restaurant downstairs, and the deposits of various urban creatures who have visited the sixteen-square-foot deck in the last decade.

It was, in other words, the least romantic thing I could think of and also the last thing I could imagine being bothered to ask for. Much like a wedding shower, come to think of it.

Thankfully, patio furniture was deemed by my sister attendants to be suitably uninspired, expensive, and difficult to wrap and thus warranted an executive bridesmaid veto. The Bride suggested a bedroom set; we settled on lingerie.

Like most things that start out as a good concept and end in humiliation—high school dances, for example—bridal showers are often organized around a theme that the bridesmaids must conceive, develop, and stringently enforce.

It is one of the cruel twists of female life that you can demand a specific list of presents only if you simultaneously agree to parade yourself around dressed up as a virginal cupcake, and while brides rightfully relish this opportunity, I live in constant bitterness that I cannot similarly declare my next birthday to be shoe-themed, therefore requiring all of my friends to pony up for a closetful of new heels.

Bridesmaids are rarely asked to help the bride acquire truly necessary items, like stilettos, but rather to create a surplus in her fantasy world—one that boasts a perfectly stocked kitchen and a thrilling boudoir.

For my friend's shower, I was given a piece of paper with The Bride's measurements and found myself spending an afternoon contemplating how she would look in flagrante delicto in a variety of expensive lacy accoutrements. On the day of, she unwrapped enough underwear to pull off a solo Victoria's Secret lingerie show, encouraged by the earnest nods of her friends and co-workers, who confirmed to one another knowingly, "He's really going to like that one."

The absurdity of outfitting a friend like a high-class call girl is not to be acknowledged by polite bridesmaids, who must steadfastly ignore the fact that in real life the bride wears flannel jammies and shouldn't be able to keep a straight face wearing white down the aisle, let alone in the sack.

To this day, I can't help but imagine my friend walking seductively into her marital bedroom wearing nothing but five inches of black silk and whispering softly into her husband's ear, "This one's from your mom."

TOIL OF OLÉ

Jodie G. woke up on the morning of her childhood friend's bridal shower hungover and already running late. The party was being held at a cottage several hours outside the city, and she knew there was no way to get there on time. It was the sixth in a string of pre-wedding happenings, and this bridesmaid had learned that the bride's mother hewed to strict schedules and unbending etiquette. Punctuality is a virtue brides are told to look for in their wedding attendants, and being late (even with a good reason like having just enjoyed a wicked night of draft beer and karaoke) is classic Bad Bridesmaid behavior.

In an effort to appease the MOB, Jodie did a detour to pick up a case of Corona and a variety of fun summer decorations, like sombreros and fold-up paper lanterns. "I figured, how can anybody have a frown on their face when they're wearing a sombrero?" she said afterward.

Bridesmaids, though, are required to shop within the category of an Assigned Shower Theme, and any deviation, no matter how minor or well-intentioned, can cause an instantaneous demotion in the bridesmaid hierarchy. Jodie got to the cottage an hour late and saw the other guests sitting in a circle on the porch, sipping white wine spritzers and nibbling hors d'oeuvres in "perfect wedding shower formation." The other bridesmaids kept pads of paper in their laps, jotting down notes as The Bride and her mother held court.

Jodie jumped out of the car and ran over to the group, arms laden with all the goodies she had brought to make up for her tardiness. Laughing and making jokes, she began decorating the porch—hanging streamers and handing out sombreros to the guests.

"About halfway through putting hats on people, I kind of looked out of the corner of my eye and I was getting the devil's look from the Mother of the Bride," Jodie remembered. "I could tell everyone was dying to play along but they knew it was better to side with Mom."

In another setting, this sort of behavior would have been the stuff of fond female memories—a demonstration of individuality and humor that spoke to the intimacy of friendship. Jodie knew, though, that none of the other bridesmaids was going to risk "misbehaving" and take her side. The theme for this shower was clearly not Mexican fiesta, but WASP.

She glanced around and saw finger sandwiches with their crusts cut off and perfect pink decorations, a table overflowing with crisply wrapped packages, and the other guests uniformly outfitted in sweater sets and heels. "And I came and ruined it," Jodie said. "If it was any other kind of party that I was going to, it would have gone over like a really fun additive. I would have been a hero."

GOING DUTCH

The bridal shower had its beginnings in an act of sixteenth-century Good Samaritan sisterhood, when the community of a dowryless bride-to-be in Holland chipped in for gifts that would allow her and her low-income husband to set off on their own, free from Daddy's fiscal clutches.

The beauty of the shower lay in its pure intentions. The bride had not asked for anything, but her friends were motivated by personal kindness to ensure that she had all the mortars and pestles she needed to set out on her new life, grinding chicken bones for her hubby with a medieval tool that now retails at Williams-Sonoma for $79.95.

It was not until the late nineteenth century that bridal showers were documented in the United States. Initially thrown by rich women in urban areas, the showers swept across North America like the Depression. Bridal registries soon followed, beginning with the Marshall Field's department store in 1924 and gaining steam from boutique to chain stores as the public developed a taste for personalized china patterns and light pink KitchenAids.

Unlike the young Dutch woman to whom the shower tradition can supposedly be traced, the beneficiaries of the modern events often do not actually need much help stocking their pantries. Nowadays, the average bride weds at twenty-seven, an age at which, one hopes, she has not only moved out of her parents' home but has managed to procure her own stemware and bedsheets. Who needs a hope chest when you have a twenty-thousand-dollar line of credit?

Armed with finely honed shopping skills and wish lists as long as their bank statements, many brides now approach their showers as though they've entered the sweepstakes lottery, expecting their bridesmaids to arrange for the jackpot. One bride e-mailed her bridesmaids instructing them not to buy her individual shower gifts, but instead to chip in for a stainless steel barbeque. They were still told to host a themed shower for the rest of the guests, however, and The Bride insisted on inviting almost every woman who would be at the wedding, all the better to maximize her haul.

"At the end of the shower, her mom said, 'Oh, look how we cleaned up,'" said Beatrice R., one of the first-time bridesmaids who had planned, hosted, and paid for the shower of her college friend. "All the guests were still there when she said it. It was very tacky."

It is completely aboveboard, or so it seems, for brides to register for everything from his and hers iPods to home entertainment systems. I'm sure it is only a matter of time before someone registers for a car and asks her bridesmaids to make down payments—or before I snap and get engaged just so I can make people buy me a puppy.

On top of the presents, bridesmaids are also expected to orchestrate an afternoon of festivities to rival the wedding itself. Meals, munchies, a fully stocked bar, and an appropriately decorated venue are all on the to-do list. Two California bridesmaids found themselves in the glare of the MOB after the shower they hosted was over. They had dutifully organized a country club brunch for thirty-five female friends and family members and had even arrived early to decorate with the streamers, balloons, and other festive paraphernalia they had bought.

By the time the brunch began, though, only seven people had shown up, including The Bride, her mother, the two bridesmaids, and two friends they had forced to come along.

"We spent $250 on party favors for seven people," said Courtney L., who has been a bridesmaid four times. The expense was nothing compared with the abuse they endured from the MOB. Originally, The Bride had wanted her shower on a specific Saturday, one that coincided with the beginning of the two bridesmaids' exam schedules. When they politely explained this and asked to reschedule, they received a "disappointed" phone call from their friend's mother, asking why they couldn't accommodate her request.

At the shower itself, the MOB did not acknowledge either woman's existence until it was time to go home—not an easy thing to do when you can easily count your lunch companions. She ignored them through the course of the event, and they passed the time drinking champagne and orange juice to keep their spirits up. Two hours later the gifts had been exchanged and the meal finished, and finally the MOB deigned to address her hosts. The bill had been delivered, and the bridesmaids were reaching to take it when the MOB sniffed, "No no, I'll get it."

"But in a polite way, like a courtesy offer," Courtney said. "Our friends are looking at us, like, 'Let her take the bill.'" Instead of graciously insisting that she would pick up the tab, the MOB turned to her daughter and commented on how the two young women were trying to show her up. She snatched up the billfold and pulled out her husband's credit card.

"Then she opens up the bill and says, 'Oh my gosh, how many mimosas did you guys drink?'" Courtney said.

As if that weren't embarrassing enough for the bridesmaid hosts, the women had another run-in with the meanie MOB in the parking lot, as they were loading her daughter's gifts into her car. Both of the bridesmaids had driven to the country club in their own vehicles, one an Audi and the other a Cadillac.

"She walks out and says, 'Are these your cars?'" Courtney remembered.

The girls said yes, and waited for her to say, "How nice, and thank you for all of your efforts today." Instead, the woman gave them a withering stare and climbed into her own car, taking one last parting shot as she turned to leave.

"Maybe I should have let you pay," she sneered.

DRESSED DOWN

The modern bridal shower requires women to shell out for almost anything their betrothed friend desires, but it is regarded as unseemly (vis-à-vis popular wedding etiquette) for the bride's family to make those demands directly. Bridesmaids, then, are really nothing more than a human buffer between the bride and her unreasonably high demands—and heaven forbid they refuse to act accordingly.

Bailey S. was in a wedding where The Bride reacted with unadulterated contempt at the shower that had been thrown in her honor. "She freaked out, because in her head it wasn't right," the four-time bridesmaid remembered.

The shower was a surprise party, and The Bride burst into tears when she showed up, but not because she was overcome with happiness. She did not have on the "perfect pink dress" she had always imagined wearing to her wedding shower, and was horrified that she had been tricked into arriving unprepared. To make matters worse, the shower was held in the home of The Bride's mother. None of the bridesmaids lived in her hometown, so they were faced with the choice of having the party at her family's home, renting a hall, or inviting fifty guests back to their hotel room. It just seemed to make sense to have it at the MOB's house, where the guests would have room to relax and the caterers could do their thing without operating out of a bathroom or broom closet.

To make life easy on Mom, the attendants had taken care of every detail, from the caterer to the flowers and decorations, and The Bride's family never had to lift a finger or even open the door to guests. The Bride, however, saw her family's involvement in her shower as a faux pas of the highest degree.

"She thought it looked terrible that her mom would be hosting her own bridal shower," Bailey said. "She said we had humiliated her."

The Bride said her mother was not to blame, even though she presumably knew the event was taking place in her own living room. The bridesmaids, though, were chastised for taking liberties with the way the shower was planned, from its inappropriate venue to the fact that they had sprung it on her unawares.

"Her buzzword was *etiquette, etiquette, etiquette*," Bailey said. "It became code for, 'You screwed up.'"

Going to showers really shouldn't be as painful as being forced into basic training or fat camp. What could be so bad about getting together with the girls on a sunny Saturday and cracking open a bottle of champagne at noon? The problem is that unlike other forms of organized torture, shower season lasts as long as you have friends who are getting married, which for most of us means at least from the ages of twenty-one to thirty-five.

It is, therefore, easy to develop a case of Shower Burn, the gradual fraying of nerves that develops from losing every weekend of your twenties to the black hole of Wedding Season.

Helpful bridesmaids are meant to spend the shower taking dictation on who bought which gift for the bride, refilling snack trays, and cleaning up discarded wrapping paper. They should carefully thread the ribbon from each gift through a ring of cardboard to construct a fake bouquet—or, alternatively, wrap the decorations around their own necks until they fall into blissful unconsciousness.

There is no good excuse to skip out on a bridal shower—whether it's work, distance, or stringent bail conditions—your absence will be regarded as a personal affront to the bride, her family, and the future of her marital union.

Talia B., a first-time bridesmaid, had already organized one expensive shower for her friend in the months leading up to the wedding. The betrothed was a dance instructor, and when a handful of her adult students approached the bridesmaids about throwing their own event, Talia and her cohorts believed they would be given a much needed respite.

"We thought, great, go ahead," she said. The women assumed that they would not have to go to the second shower, or be responsible for any aspect of its success. It was to be held at a restaurant, where guests would enjoy drinks, appetizers, and a main course as The Bride opened her gifts. The bridesmaids were invited after all, and they relished a day where they would not have to clean up or be in charge. When the check came, though, the other hosts freaked out. "These ladies decided they didn't want to pay for it," Talia said, "so we had to foot the bill at the last moment."

Even if you don't have to throw down your American Express at every event, attending multiple showers can leave bridesmaids spent. Sarah G. was forced to attend three bridal blowouts held for the woman she had met on vacation and who unexpectedly asked her to be a bridesmaid. She came to each party knowing no one but The Bride, and had to explain to each guest who she was and why she was there. "Usually when you go to a shower, there are your old friends or your close friends, so it might not be great fun but you can go and chat and whatever," she said. "Imagine having to put a huge amount of effort into it, and meet people and introduce yourself."

When the other bridesmaids and guests would ask where she came from, Sarah had to patiently explain that she had met The Bride just recently in Mexico. Then she would turn around and whisper under her breath, "And where am I never going again? Mexico."

LET'S MAKE A RAW DEAL

The main responsibility of bridesmaids once the shower is actually in full swing is to give the appearance that the event is not just another cash-grab but a grand occasion for everyone involved. It may be tempting to just let people show up, dump their presents on the table, knock back a couple shots of vodka, and head for the door, but wedding showers are supposed to be micromanaged festivals of fun.

And there can be no fun without games.

Of all the attendants' duties, making up shower activities has the potential to be one of the more entertaining bridesmaid tasks. Imagine a rousing session of Pin the Pre-Nup on the Groom, or an engagement obstacle course where women must jump over career hurdles, change into revealing outfits, and drain a martini while saying something charming before dashing to a finish line decorated to look like an altar.

Alas, the games bridesmaids referee are usually simple tests of knowledge for the bride-to-be to ace. They are also meant to celebrate the magic of marriage or to establish whether the bride is equipped to perform her womanly duties. One etiquette Web site suggests sticking to topics such as "food and travel." Right, because most women spend their lives creating original recipes and jet-setting around the world.

At my friend's shower, we had constructed a sort of Dating Game questionnaire—a pretty standard bridal shower pastime, according to various Web sites and bridal guides. The groom had been e-mailed a series of questions, and I had written his responses on blue cue cards. At the shower, we asked The Bride the same set of questions and scored her ability to match his answers. Mensa-worthy it was not.

I had not yet been branded All Bad, so the other bridesmaids felt comfortable assigning me the task of e-mailing the groom. After a mind-numbing brainstorming session, I sent him a list of seemingly innocuous questions ranging from the enlightening "What's your favorite meal?" to the brain-tickling "Who designed The Bride's dress?"

Feeling like the questions were a little tame, I added, "How many carats is the ring?" It seemed harmless enough. I had heard the answer on at least four different occasions as The Bride showed off her new bauble (referred to as "My precious") to me and anyone else who happened to find themselves in its glare. When the groom wrote back, he declined to answer the question and typed "That's inappropriate," instead.

When I shared this story at the shower I was met with stares of disbelief. It was as if I had admitted asking him his annual salary or penis size.

"Oh my God!" the other bridesmaids squealed as The Bride rolled her eyes.

I see now that asking the groom about the ring is tacky, while asking a friend to gift-wrap a G-string and present it in front of the groom's mother is normal and civilized behavior.

But at least at my friend's shower, both bride and groom knew the answer to my question. Barbara D. attended a party where The Bride failed the quiz she was given, surely a bad omen for any marriage.

"We had asked the groom a bunch of questions, and on the day of the shower we asked her the same ones. You know, to imply how well they knew each other," said Barbara, a five-timer. "She didn't get a single one of them right. Not one. Every single one was so far off, it was painful."

The bridesmaids tried to call the game off, but The Bride was oblivious to the awkward situation she was creating at her own shower.

"It was so embarrassing. His mother was like, 'Um, what's going on?'" said Barbara. "They just got divorced."

It can be somewhat funny when brides fail miserably at the games they are given, but the end rarely justifies the means. Julia D. went to a shower with her fellow wedding attendants and was greeted at the door by Über Brides-maid, a woman who "just makes you want to throw up, she's so excited."

The ecstatic organizer handed Julia and two other women ribbons that they were instructed to tie around their wrists. The guests were supposed to collect as many of the ribbons as possible during the course of the shower, and would receive one every time they pointed out a woman crossing her legs. Let us pause for a moment to reflect on how silly this game really is. Is staring into another woman's lap really the best way to test a person's skills of observation? Or would it just have been too easy to collect ribbons every time someone checked their watch to see if it was almost time to leave?

"It was supposed to be a bonding thing," Julia said. Über Bridesmaid explained that the woman who won would receive a prize, and Julia imagined a free facial or perhaps a loot bag stuffed with makeup. The prize was a mug.

That exercise was only the beginning of Julia's trauma. It seems Über Bridesmaid was well versed in the history of wedding shower games, and had planned, so to speak, to kick it old school.

Until the 1970s, bridal showers were as much indoctri-nation sessions as they were celebrations. The parties were meant to underscore the importance of getting married, especially for the single gals in attendance. To this end, many games were designed to "give hope" to those who were not yet hooked up, and to encourage them into the marriage fold.

At the shower Julia attended, the bridesmaids and other guests were placed in a circle and asked to take turns giving The Bride advice on how to have a long and happy marriage.

Get a group of women together under normal circumstances and ask them how to have a successful relationship, and inevitably someone will make a blow-job joke, someone else will praise the virtues of separate bank accounts, and another woman will suggest the ingestion of prescription narcotics.

Humor has no place at most bridal showers.

"Nothing about sex ever came up," Julia said. "Everyone was like, 'Be supportive, be honest, talk things out, respect one another.' All of that trite bullshit."

When it came time for Julia and her two friends to participate, all three of them passed. They were not married, they explained, so couldn't possibly offer any helpful advice. Julia and one of her friends were graciously allowed to skip their turn, but by the time the third conscientious objector had declined to participate, Über Bridesmaid was, to put it mildly, Über Pissed. In an effort to defend herself, Julia's friend informed the group that she had just broken up with a boyfriend and wasn't dating, so she wasn't in the best frame of mind to offer relationship advice.

"So this bridesmaid says, 'Okay, why don't you give her advice on how not to drive a man away,'" Julia remembered. Many of the guests started howling with laughter, but the newly dumped bridesmaid and her friends were stunned.

To make matters worse, Über Bridesmaid thought the game was so successful she would go around the circle a second time. "We were all like, don't you even look at me," Julia said.

STRAIGHT UP WITH A TWIST

Watching a grown woman tear open gifts and play boring games is considerably—although not completely—less painful when you have a drink in your hand. Sadly, however, the combination of women, booze, and bridal talk does not always fly.

I spent the majority of the night after my friend's shower lying on my kitchen floor praying for death and calling my boyfriend on my cell phone to come downstairs and pour water on my face. If bridal showers take that kind of toll on me, imagine what they do to the older women in attendance.

Christie B. attended a bridal shower at the house of a betrothed friend who lived with her parents, sister, and grandmother, known as Nana. "It's also a family that doesn't drink very much," Christie explained.

The bridesmaid who was in charge of refreshments was not familiar with her hosts' ways, and when the elderly Nana asked for a dash of sherry, she was given a generous drink.

"The bridesmaid poured Nana a huge wineglass full, and because no one there really drinks, no one realizes you're not supposed to pour that much sherry," said Christie. "And Nana's, like, one foot in the retirement home."

An hour later, another bridesmaid noticed that Nana's glass was empty and poured her another drink.

"So we're in the middle of the shower, and The Bride's unwrapping her presents and Nana just slumps over in her chair," Christie said. "She's passed out totally dead drunk."

It was quickly determined that Grandma was not actually dead, and The Bride's father was called in to carry the unconscious old woman upstairs to bed. The bridesmaids consulted one another and realized that a ninety-year-old woman who weighs approximately ninety-five pounds had probably consumed the equivalent of about five stiff drinks.

"At the end of the shower she comes back down and says, 'Are you going to open your presents now, dear?'" Christie remembered. "She thought she had just gone for a little nap."

GUEST LISTLESS

If I were a ninety-year-old woman, I might have chugged that sherry just to get out of watching any more gifts being opened. Sometimes even the Best Bridesmaids require a strong cocktail, usually after the shower's reigning queen tells them they failed to live up to her expectations.

Chelsea K. had planned to host a couples shower at her house in the country. The wedding party had agreed to a date in July and a guest list of about six couples. "The party was going to be a casual day of swimming and BBQ-ing with close friends," Chelsea remembered. "The Bride said she was thrilled to have a relaxed weekend before the hectic wedding schedule began."

Two months before the planned shower, Chelsea asked for a list of the names and e-mail addresses of the people The Bride wanted to invite. "When I didn't receive the list, I asked again, and again and again," she said. "Finally, The Bride left me a hard copy document—nine pages in length—with the name of every wedding guest on it. 'Don't worry,' she said, 'I've highlighted the ones to contact for the party.'"

The highlighted list included thirty-six couples, ranging from current and former work colleagues to out-of-town relatives. Chelsea freaked out at the prospect of having seventy-two people at her country house, and threatened to cancel the whole thing. The Bride was not about to accept any responsibility for the matter. "She blamed me for pressuring her to produce the list on such 'short notice,'" the bridesmaid recalled. "She said she had wanted to talk to me about the guest list a month earlier, but that it would have been bad etiquette to give it to me without a formal request."

It was the bridesmaid who was being bad, apparently, even though The Bride had wanted to invite half of her graduating class to a shower meant for twelve.

Bridesmaids rarely escape a shower unscathed by such insults or indignation. I left ours hopelessly drunk from sipping champagne cocktails since noon, all the better to forget the fact that I had spent half of my rent in a single day. But while a regular hangover wears off, the residual pain of Shower Burn can be hard to shake. Even my bride-to-be mentioned in the days after her own party that she was dreading attending another woman's shower in the weeks to come.

"I don't want to go. I hate wedding showers," she said, sighing. "Except for mine. Mine was fun."

5

THE BACHELORETTE
COMPLEX

Get a sober driver or bus and you are on your way to either one or multiple bar stops. Have the bride get a little tipsy and take lots of pictures!

—*www.bachelorettepartyideas.net*

Hiring a stripper was never an option for my former friend's bachelorette party. There had been, you see, a couple of "incidents" when we were in college, and our group was unanimously scarred by the thought of paying for another glimpse of greased-up male nudity. The first damaging experience occurred at a birthday party that I didn't attend, where a male stripper had reportedly given a somewhat lackluster performance. We'd gone to school in a small town, which meant occasional public sightings of the decidedly unsexy stripper when we went for coffee or drinks downtown. Once he was spotted, members of his former audience would grip my arm and avert their eyes, trying hard not to picture him naked, as I imagined this sleazy-looking man in tear-away pants actually tearing away his pants.

The other close encounter of the lurid kind came during a road trip to the city for a friend's birthday. We went to a male strip club after taking in a performance of *Les Miserables*, a unique blend of high culture and low—Jean Valjean with a chaser of Lance Stallion.

Inside the club, groups of chain-smoking middle-aged women occupied a cluster of small, dirty tables, and our group of rowdy twentysomethings was ushered into a corner beside the bar and instructed to remain behind a wooden partition that separated us from the stage. We drank vodka and sodas inside our holding pen and laughed as a steroid-riddled dancer in a hot pink G-string shook his manhood in the birthday girl's face, both of her hands plastered firmly over her eyes. Onstage, a stripper was gyrating inside a glass stall, and women paid to go up and hose him down with a shower nozzle. At one point he flipped himself upside-down, the force of gravity overpowering his own obvious excitement. Needless to say, once you've seen a naked man doing a handstand, the desire to hire a stripper fades like a junkie's libido.

Our friend's country weekend retreat, therefore, involved no men at all, save those on the pages of the trashy magazines we read poolside during the day. This relaxed, raunch-free take on the bachelorette party is definitely not the norm. Most women believe they are meant to live up to the mythical standard of the male stag party, the much-talked-about (but rarely realized) evening of hot nudity, flowing booze, and rock star partying. In the 1985 Tom Hanks film *Bachelor Party*, a friend of the shaggy haired, pre-*Philadelphia*, post–*Bosom Buddies* Hanks requests an event filled with "chicks and guns and fire trucks and hookers and booze! All the things that make life worth living." Despite the fact that Hanks's evening also involved sex with prostitutes and a donkey overdosing on cocaine and pills, this is the model women strive to achieve (usually minus the guns and whores).

According to www.bachelorette.com, only about 20 percent of bachelorette parties hire a stripper, but if the events are organized around the things that make women's lives worth living, then our gender is seemingly all about stretch limos, blender drinks, tiaras, inappropriately shaped pasta, and LifeSavers candy. And it has fallen to the bridesmaids to transform their love-struck single girl into a raging veil-clad hootchie clutching a penis-shaped straw in her sweaty hands.

HALF-COCKED

Unlike men, most women do not get sexually aroused by watching the opposite sex perform a striptease. Some people say this is because we are turned on by nonvisual stimulants, such as conversation, emotional connection, and money. I believe there is a less cerebral explanation: many male strippers are distinctly unattractive, and the proximity to swinging male genitalia is enough to make even the straightest girl rethink her own sexual preference.

When she was a twenty-four-year-old bridesmaid virgin, Kaitlyn P. invited a stripper to perform at the apartment she shared with her mother, the most liberal of the bridesmaids' parents. None of the girls had her own place at the time, and there were no male strip clubs in the city where the bridal party lived, which is unfortunate, because going to the strip club is always preferable to bringing the strip club to you.

Still, since Kaitlyn's friend had been raised by her Catholic family to have a healthy fear of alcohol and adult situations to begin with, her bridal party agreed that she would be adequately traumatized by a private showing.

Despite her modest tastes, the blushing bride did have one major vice: police officers. The fact that she is aroused by men who can punish her probably has a lot to do with her religion's punitive view toward sex, but her friends left the psychoanalysis at home and just gave the girl what she wanted. The bridesmaids thumbed dutifully through the phone book, looking for Hot Man Action in between ads for Hotels and Housing Inspectors. Kaitlyn found a company that offered male dancers in a variety of costumes— from cop to robber—but that strangely also hired out birthday party entertainment and magicians. She momentarily considered hiring a clown to make X-rated balloon art, but ended up settling for Officer Steve.

The theme of the bachelorette evening was "Cougar Lounge Party," the apartment decorated with leopard-print pillows and magenta streamers, and the guests dressed up like the cast of *Charlie's Angels* after two decades of drug abuse and bad relationships. The bridal party had invited The Bride early to lubricate her with alcohol, but she arrived only half an hour before "the talent" was scheduled to show, and Kaitlyn worried that she "couldn't get her to knock enough back to thoroughly enjoy the experience."

The Bride was still in the dark about the night's surprise attraction, so the friends all sat around in their tight pants and bustiers making polite conversation, as though gathered for an innocent yet strangely themed potluck dinner. Kaitlyn and the other bridesmaids were silently draining shots of vodka when there was a knock at the door. Although they weren't actually playing music, a man's voice identified himself as a police officer and informed them that there had been several "noise complaints," his bellows ringing through the deathly quiet apartment. The Bride was dispatched to open the door, where she found a middle-aged man in a police uniform standing in the hall. She dutifully led the stripper into the apartment, where the wedding party watched as he set up his oversized ghetto blaster and rearranged the furniture.

"It was awkwardly quiet," Kaitlyn said. "We just sat there and stared at him."

Officer Steve was in his early forties, Kaitlyn guessed, at least fifteen years older than the women for whom he was stripping and only moderately younger than the host's mother, who was watching the proceedings with a look of disgust from her seat at the dining room table.

"He looked like something off a soap opera, like Bo on *Days of Our Lives*," said Kaitlyn. "He was very chiseled and he seemed very uncomfortable."

Eventually, The Bride was handcuffed to a chair in the middle of the room and Officer Steve began grinding his body against her, to the soothing beats of Rick Astley emanating from his ghetto blaster. Suddenly, much to The Bride's terror, he tore off his police uniform, exposing a large orange G-string, which hit the floor a few seconds later.

"We weren't really prepared for the horror of it," said Kaitlyn, "and how raunchy it was going to be. He took everything off and got right up in it." The host herself continued drinking heavily, reasoning that if no one was having a good time, at least she wouldn't remember it in the morning.

The Bride remained a good sport, but the rest of the party sat in shocked silence, unwilling witnesses to middle-aged nudity. To make matters worse, the air-conditioning was on the fritz and the apartment was sweltering, causing beads of sweat to form on parts of the male anatomy that are unattractive even when dry. After dancing (if you could call it that) to just two songs on his outdated mix tape—a performance that lasted less than ten minutes— he abruptly ended the show and walked into a corner of the living room to put his uniform back on. Unsure of the proper etiquette in such a situation, the ladies offered him dinner, and he picked over the plates of salad, cheese, and vegetarian lasagna that littered the table.

An obviously tipsy Kaitlyn collected $150 from her friends and escorted Officer Steve back out into the hall-way to pay him and send him on his crime-fighting and ass-shaking way. He handed her his business card, a small headshot lifted from one of those charity firemen calendars, and commented appraisingly on the tight purple velvet pants she was wearing. Then, perhaps in an effort to regain a degree of his dignity, the stripper lifted Kaitlyn up and enveloped her in a big wet kiss.

"He just started mauling me outside the door," she remembered.

As luck would have it, at that very moment The Bride's two Catholic sisters emerged from an elevator down the hall to see their host in the grip of a middle-aged cop, his uniform disheveled and a boom box resting at his feet. When The Bride found out that her best friend had swapped spit with a stripper, she proceeded to drink so much that she blacked out.

"I think she was just stunned," Kaitlyn said of her friend's response to the bachelorette party. "We never spoke about it ever again."

FULLY COCKED

Seeing an older man take it all off is probably not as permanently damaging as imagining a family member naked—at least for most people.

Mary Beth K. attended a bachelorette party where the groom's sister, a fellow bridesmaid, had come up with a disturbing game for the women to play. It was a take on the childhood favorite Pin the Tail on the Donkey, only in this case, the donkey was the groom and the "tail" wasn't pinned to his bum. It wasn't a tail, either.

The groom's sister had found a picture of her betrothed brother buck naked, taken to memorialize a nasty sunburn he had endured on a family vacation. In the photo, he was covering himself with one hand while holding the other to his mouth in a gesture of mock surprise. She had it blown up to almost life-size, and instructed the female guests—including the Mother of the Bride—to draw a penis on a sheet of scrap paper and cut it out with scissors before the game began.

"I thought it was kind of gross," Mary Beth said, "but we did it anyway."

The Bride's mother, who is divorced and obviously does not have the most optimistic view of men, drew "the smallest penis you've ever seen," according to Mary Beth, much to the delight of the other guests and the potential trauma of her daughter. The groom's sister, however, had a more generous outlook on her family jewels.

"The sister drew a big one," she said. "It was really bizarre."

LIVE RUDE GIRLS

Bachelorette parties, like their human equivalent Paris Hilton, are a child of the 1980s. According to Beth Montemurro, who studies the phenomenon in her book *Something Old, Something Bold*, the events were first mentioned in an academic paper written in 1985 by a woman researching female attendance at strip clubs. The first newspaper article to report on the parties appeared in the *Chicago Sun Times* in 1988, penned by none other than Richard Roeper, he of the eagerly administered thumbs-up. His article, which ran under the headline HEY, BACHELORETTES CAN ACT SLEAZY, TOO, related stories of women drinking excessively, partaking in frank discussions of sex, and being entertained by strippers—and one assumes he gave the trend an enthusiastic review.

The parties may not be steeped in history or dignity, but they have become a required rite of passage for women and another mandatory event planned by busy bridesmaids. Men may be able to head out on the town with nothing but a dime bag and a wallet full of dollar bills, but women must plan the ultimate Girls' Night Out.

Sylvanna N. attended a bachelorette party for her best friend that was an expensive, classy, and formally attired night on the town—exactly the opposite of what The Bride had requested. The event was the brainchild of Gayle, a Bad Bridesmaid in the evil sense of the term, who ignored The Bride's preference for Kentucky Fried Chicken and dive bars and planned the evening to reflect her own highly refined tastes.

Sylvanna and the other guests were invited to a hotel, where they would be spending the night post-festivities. The boutique establishment was highly modern, coldly designed, and populated by guests who probably believed that White Castle was the name of Diddy's Hamptons estate. Sylvanna walked into the stark, minimalist lobby and was greeted by an austere receptionist wearing an outfit that she estimates had the same dollar value as her own monthly mortgage payments. After registering, the bridesmaid was led through three different checkpoints, where her ID was scrutinized and her room keycard swiped.

"I haven't had to deal with this level of security at the airport," she said.

When she walked into the room, Sylvanna saw rugs, sheets, tables, chairs, and even curtains a blinding shade of virginal white. Just the kind of place where you want to get good and loaded on red wine.

Gayle, on the other hand, gushed over the "tasteful, elegant" décor and scurried around the room inspecting the white accoutrements as the rest of the bridal party searched their handbags for shades. The Bride showed up a few minutes later looking irate. "I practically had to go through a strip search down there!" she told her friends.

After a few warm-up cocktails, the women headed out on the town, bypassing the sleazy bar The Bride had wanted to visit and instead lining up outside a pick-up joint for the rich and available.

"The entire evening Gayle approached various good-looking, well-dressed young men—not, of course, before deciding whether or not they 'looked rich,'" Sylvanna remembered. The bachelorette party the Bad Bridesmaid had planned was not a chance for The Bride to sow her wild oats, but rather an intricate ruse for Gayle to score herself a man. The other bridesmaids encouraged her in her cruising, buying her drink after drink and sending her off after eligible bachelors as they plotted their escape.

"She proceeded to get completely wasted and tell everyone in the bar that she was looking to get married, that she wanted to be rich, and that she came from money so they would be lucky to get her," Sylvanna remembered.

Finally, Gayle was so drunk that the rest of the party had to take her back to the hotel, depositing her unconscious frame on the white bed that they hoped she would befoul in an unclassy way.

"Then we left her and went to the townie bar and the strip club," Sylvanna said, "just like the bride wanted."

Of course, not every engaged woman wants a simple party with her friends. Creative (and wealthy) bridesmaids may elect to plan the ultimate girls' getaway, spending thousands on limousines, caterers, private clubs, and matching outfits for themselves and the bride. And why stop there? Destination bachelorette parties have become popular recently, and bridal groups are as common a sight in Vegas as Midwesterners on vacation from morality.

Inga S. and the rest of the bridal party took their friend on a surprise weekend trip to Las Vegas for her bachelorette weekend, but they were unprepared for post-9/11 security issues. They had booked the airfare and reserved a hotel suite, and on a warm summer Friday afternoon they put their plan into action. The bridesmaids had not even told The Bride's fiancé where they were headed because they wanted to catch her completely off guard. It turned out their plan worked a little bit too well.

As their friend left work they grabbed her, blindfolded her with a stylish silk scarf, and shoved her in a taxi-van to go to the airport. They had packed a bag of her things so she wouldn't have to go home, and cranked up the music in the cab so she wouldn't be able to hear the sounds of traffic or the white noise of the airport and figure out what was up.

Understandably, perhaps, The Bride began to get nervous. "She starts panicking because she thinks we're going to leave her somewhere," Inga said. The women tried to calm her down without completely ruining the surprise they had so carefully planned, reassuring her that they were not going to take her to the woods and leave her for dead. When they arrived at the airport and successfully made their way to the check-in counter, an airline employee noticed that the blindfolded girl was somewhat distraught and refused to check her in or let her on the plane until she was thoroughly interrogated by security personnel.

"I have to know that she wants to be a part of this," the employee explained, in the tone of a woman who just does not get paid enough to deal with this shit.

Luckily, The Bride recovered her poise before she was forced to endure a full body-cavity search.

POLE-R OPPOSITES

The bride can refuse to partake in her forced kidnapping, or to do body shots off a chiseled bartender, but bridesmaids must throw themselves into the event with abandon, whether that involves a last-minute plane ride or a pricey bar tab.

Ella H. declined an invitation to her friend's bachelorette party because she was low on funds and doesn't drink, thinking that combo would make her a bit of a buzz kill on a night of debauchery. One bridesmaid suggested that she just come for the first hour and say hello to The Bride, to avoid hurting her feelings. Ella agreed and took a cab to meet the bachelorette party at one of the many bars they visited over the course of the night. She stayed for less than an hour and drank a soda while the other girls tossed back shooters and swilled cocktails.

A few days later, another bridesmaid called Ella and instructed her to "pay up" for her share of the evening. The woman claimed she owed 15 percent of the total cost of alcohol, food, bar cover charges, hotel room, and limo. Ella protested, but her logic was met with a hostile rebuttal.

"She said, 'If you show up, you pay up!'" the bridesmaid recalled. "So I did."

Thirty-two-year-old two-time bridesmaid Hailey P., meanwhile, got in trouble with her friend The Bride after she resisted a bachelorette party plan to take a pole-dancing class. The outing involves a group of women learning how to swing around a metal stripper pole, courtesy of a private instructor. Considered a challenging workout by celebrities and crack whores alike, stripping is an increasingly popular bachelorette party activity. But Hailey, a mother of two who has mounted only one pole in her life, was not comfortable with the idea of unleashing her inner Demi Moore.

"I think of the connotations of pole dancing and I'm like, yuck, gross me out," said Hailey. "You're just grinding up against a giant phallic object."

The rest of the frisky bridesmaids were dead set on pole dancing, as was The Bride, and they were unmoved by Hailey's objections. If a bridesmaid is asked to swing around a greasy pole, she is expected to reply, "How high?"

"I guess you're supposed to be wild and crazy for your bachelorette, but it's peer pressure," she said. "I don't want to be forced into this kind of a situation."

Instead of grinning and bearing it, the Bad Bridesmaid complained about the plan on a personal Web log, one that The Bride would read on a regular basis. The posting was met with anger and plenty of choice words for Hailey, who received a phone call from The Bride immediately and was berated for being close-minded and judgmental. The two eventually sorted things out, but this Bad Bridesmaid was unprepared for the other angry responses she received, flung at her through cyberspace from people not even involved in the wedding party.

"I got some really nasty replies from pole-dancing instructors," she said. "I have no idea how they found my blog."

DRUNK AND DISORDERLY

The most dangerous aspect of the modern bachelorette party—besides the likelihood of choking on one of the phallic hors d'oeuvres or party favors—is the fact that booze flows at these things like sweat off an old stripper's back. Bridesmaids have to maintain an attitude of happy obedience during the engagement period, and nothing gets the pent-up complaints flowing like a few shots of Sex on the Beach and a six-pack of wine coolers.

At a friend's bachelorette party, Jacqueline K. was told to show up wearing an awful bridesmaid dress bought from a secondhand store or vintage shop. Normally a woman with exquisite taste, Jacqueline found a hideous dress of layered tulle with an unflattering bustline. On the night of the bachelorette, the guests showed up in an array of ugly outfits and howled with laughter at each other's picks. Until, that is, one of the bridesmaids informed them they were going out in public. Jacqueline had assumed they were staying at the host's apartment and would only be made fun of by one another. Faced with the prospect of being seen by perfect strangers wearing a dress that should have been destroyed on principle, Jacqueline drowned her inhibitions in alcohol, getting so drunk that The Bride herself eventually had to escort her out of the bar.

Five-timer Helena L. got so wasted at another bachelorette party that she actually told The Bride off for her "unladylike" behavior. The bridal party had hired a bus to drive them around town from bar to bar, drinking all the way. They wore matching tank tops that read BRIDESMAIDS GONE WILD and were having a great time, but all that alcohol fueled a confrontational streak Helena didn't know she had.

When they stumbled home from their night on the town, The Bride immediately headed upstairs to vomit, and Helena thought it would be a good time to inform her that a surprise shower was planned for the next day. She walked into the bathroom where The Bride was crouched over the toilet and began shaking her, slurring that her shower was in just a few hours and that her mother and in-laws would be in attendance.

"I told her to shape up and that basically she was a disgrace for getting that drunk," Helena remembered.

The next day, however, it was the bridesmaids who suffered for their crime of exceptionally bad bachelorette party planning, running to the bathroom every time a gift was unwrapped.

"We were basically just lying on the couch waiting for it to be over," she said. "She was opening her presents, and we were all taking turns throwing up."

Luckily for Helena, though, The Bride wasn't angry that her bachelorette party had ended with one of her bridesmaids telling her off.

She didn't remember a thing.

6

EXTREME MAKEOVER

The first rule of eye makeup is that you can never wear enough blue eye shadow.

—SHELLY DEVOTO, *My Girl*

There are a lot of things for which I will pay $100. Ten martinis, for example, although I will pay for those in more ways than one. I will shell out twice that for shoes, and currently throw down six times that price for rent each month. I have spent more on birthday gifts for friends and a whole lot more on spur-of-the-moment presents for myself.

I would not normally put down $100 to have my hair blow-dried, but when weddings are involved, price limits are strained further than control-top pantyhose. Hair accessories that usually cost fifty cents are suddenly fifty dollars, and a process that involves nothing more than hot air and a round brush is priced at the same hourly rate charged by shrinks and criminal lawyers.

Before I was dismissed from my friend's bridal party, she had already settled on the stylist who would perfect her gorgeous tresses on the wedding day, and the hairdresser had graciously offered to take care of the bridesmaids' as well—for the reasonable fee of $100. Each.

In real life, if I gave a hairdresser that much money, I'd expect to walk out with Elle McPherson's locks grafted to my scalp or $55 worth of change in my pocket. During wedding prep, though, you are not paying for the service so much as the experience of being fussed over en masse while you sip champagne and count down the final moments of your friend's single life.

In order to preserve the harmony of those last few hours, it is inadvisable to say no to the group makeover, even when the "over" part applies to how you are being charged. So, for several hours and sometimes several days before weddings, bridesmaids are subjected to the will, whim, and pricing chart of makeup artists who act like they are peddling powdered gold and pedicurists who soak your feet while fleecing your finances. Each bridesmaid is treated like a human art exhibit, which must be sculpted, painted, and polished before going on display. And there can be no art without suffering.

Or at least that's what I hear. My hair dried during the car ride to the wedding.

WIGGING OUT

Aubrey R. had completed her doctorate just a few weeks before her friend's early summer wedding, and felt like a major change was in order. She'd been stuck at her desk for weeks, literally pulling her hair out, and with her paper finished and her dissertation over, she was itching for a physical change to mark her transition from lowly student researcher to Aubrey R—, Ph.D. Like Clark Kent chucking his glasses to become Superman, or Justin Timberlake ditching N'Sync to launch his solo career, she needed a noticeable break from the past.

So, she shaved her head in an act of joyful rebellion, forgetting in one Bad Bridesmaid moment that she'd agreed to be a wedding attendant and had RSVP'd with a full head of hair. The reality of this commitment did not completely dawn on her until the day before a bridal party dinner, where she would be seeing The Bride for the first time with her skull exposed. In anticipation of the meeting, Aubrey sent a quick e-mail to her friend gently breaking the news of her baldness, saying something along the lines of, "Hi, how are you, and by the way I shaved my head."

Maybe The Bride didn't read the whole e-mail, or perhaps she thought the admission was wacky Ph.D. lingo, but in any case, there was no indication that she understood what had actually happened.

"Apparently she thought I was kidding," Aubrey said afterward.

The true punch line came at the dinner party, when Aubrey sat down to silence and looks of disbelief from the other women at the table. No one said a word about her new 'do as they nibbled on their Caesar salads and sipped their Kir Royals. The Bride simply stared, slack-jawed, for the majority of the dinner, as if Aubrey had come in with a swastika freshly carved in her forehead. It was not until the women were on their way to a bar after dinner that The Bride finally mustered the power of speech, blurting out, "Can you wear a wig?" as the other bridesmaids stifled their giggles.

"I didn't even get the chance to offer or talk about it or anything, she just asked me right away," Aubrey said.

The Bride explained that baldness did not exactly fit with the theme of her wedding, which was more princess than punk rock.

"A bridesmaid with no hair really didn't go with her vision," Aubrey recalled. "She said, 'I don't want people looking at you, I want them looking at me.'"

Fair enough, you might think—although Aubrey pointed out that people were just as likely to stare at her once she glued a mass of horse hair to her head—and in the end she conceded to the plan.

"I did it because I was doing a nice thing for my friend," she said. "I thought about whether it would compromise me, and it wouldn't, but it would really have hurt her if I hadn't done it."

Aubrey borrowed a cheap synthetic bob from her boyfriend's sister. It was a flippy, badly constructed number, but it was free and Aubrey had determined that if she was going to wear a weave, she certainly wasn't going to pay $150 for it. She'd also resolved not to care about how she looked on the day of the wedding, but soon found that she couldn't ignore the way the wig made her *feel*. Besides the psychological discomfort, the hairpiece dug into her scalp and was unbearably hot and itchy in the summer swelter. She was also terrified it was going to blow off during the wedding photographs, leaving her bare head exposed just as the shutter snapped closed.

Mercifully, the wig stayed in place through the photo shoot and for the duration of the wedding. But toward the end of the night, Aubrey could take it no more and pulled it off when most of the guests had trickled out, deciding that The Bride could not begrudge her baldness now that she was happily wed and the videographer had traded his camera for a large check and a nightcap. She pulled the bob off her head and retreated to a corner, fanning herself with the clump of hair and silently vowing her newfound respect for men who wear toupees every day. After a few minutes, she noticed a group of the remaining guests looking at her and whispering furtively. They were friends of the groom and they eventually approached her and began thanking her effusively for participating in the night.

"They started sort of awkwardly saying all these nice things to me," Aubrey said. "They thought I had cancer."

RIPPED OFF

According to the Fairchild Bridal Bank, a study of the wedding industry compiled each year by the publishers of *Bride's*, *Modern Bride*, and *Elegant Bride* magazines, American women spend $606 million each year to get themselves sculpted, sprayed, and shellacked before their weddings. The money is spent on diet books, Pilates classes, Botox sessions, emergency skin peels, and, it seems, the odd wig. Having the ultimate wedding means creating the ultimate cast of human participants, and even grooms are getting in on the act with visits to "sports spas" for a last-minute nip or pluck.

The bridal industry may target the bride first, but bridesmaids are always caught in the crossfire, coordinating their looks, from their bleached teeth to their perfect French pedicures. Who wants to be the one overweight woman in the bridal party, or be ridiculed in perpetuity for amateur-hour eye shadow and a pedestrian hairstyle? So bridesmaids, too, are paying for high-octane makeovers, spending upward of three hundred dollars for a day of mud wraps, salt scrubs, and Swedish massage. By this point in a Bad Bridesmaid's career, money has typically lost all meaning, and most decide that if they are going to the poorhouse, they might as well go in style.

Joelle H. was getting ready for her friend's summer wedding when one of the other bridesmaids went into full meltdown mode over her customized look. They were having their hair done at the hotel before the ceremony, with one hairdresser in charge of updos while the other worked the curling and flat irons, like an assembly line for Big Hair Barbie.

The bridesmaid in question had long blond tresses and had announced months earlier—on the way home from the bachelorette party, to be exact—that she would be styling it in tight ringlets. Wearing your hair curly for a formal event is about as original an idea as donning pearl earrings for a job interview or losing your virginity after the prom, but the bridesmaid decreed that the "unique" hairstyle would be hers and hers alone for the big day.

In the midst of preparations, though, two of the other girls (who had put considerably less forethought into their hairstyles) decided that they, too, would go curly. This caused the blond bridesmaid to burst into tears, and she ran to The Bride begging her to intervene, forcing her to spend the morning of her wedding convincing this text-book Bad Bridesmaid that she would still look different from the other members of the bridal party, all of whom had hair of various colors and lengths.

Now, some bridesmaids become Bad because they can't take the stress or live up to the obligations, but others are simply born that way. Bad-to-the-Bone Bridesmaids, like Joelle's co-attendant, will not sacrifice their space in the spotlight even during another woman's wedding, and will someday morph into mothers who force their children to enter beauty pageants.

Regular Bad Bridesmaids will subject themselves to an unusual degree of stress and trauma in order to look just right, but something inevitably goes horribly wrong. Razors, lasers, and tweezers are all instrumental in the quest for perfection, and malfunctions are to be expected when that much heavy machinery is in play.

A three-timer named Casey G. found herself carrying around an eighty-five-dollar foot-tall beehive for her friend's wedding. She was wearing a retro-style halter dress, and the hairdresser had decided to build her 'do into a complementary look. After what seemed like hours of back-combing and the dispensing of an entire bottle of hairspray onto the bridesmaid's head, the stylist felt that further reinforcements were required. Two full packs of bobby pins were spliced into Casey's hair, enough metal to cause a disruption in the magnetic field around the church.

After the ceremony, the pins were digging into her head and Casey decided to take them out and let her hair down for the rest of the night. She imagined a hair commercial moment: that the last pin would be set free and she would shake her head seductively, sending her hair cascading down to her shoulders like that of a naughty librarian at the end of a shift. Instead, her hairstyle stayed exactly where it had been, held in place by the expensive shellacking it had received hours earlier.

"It didn't come out," Casey said. "It was still in the exact formation, and it stayed that way all night, unsupported."

It's better to have too much hair, though, than to suddenly find yourself missing a chunk. The day before her friend's wedding, Hannah J. and the rest of the bridal party went to the salon to have their nails done and eyebrows waxed—a last-minute pampering session, a final gloss to perfect their shiny facades for the big day. As Hannah lay on the waxing chair, the serenity of the scene was interrupted by a piercing pain in her eyelid. The technician had somehow managed to rip off a layer of skin along with her wayward eyebrow hairs and Hannah wondered if reconstructive surgery would be required.

She didn't want to alarm her friend The Bride, who had never had any waxing done, so she promised her that the redness would fade by the time of the wedding. Once she was alone, Hannah rushed to inspect her ravaged eyelid in the bathroom mirror. There, she saw that underneath her perfectly arched brow, a slash of angry red flesh oozed a clear liquid.

"Of course the next day it was a scab," Hannah sighed.

Needless to say, she did not return to that salon when in need of a bikini wax.

FAKE-OUT AND BAKE

There are many dangers associated with being in a bridal party, but the role has not yet been definitively proven to give people cancer, although I am convinced that all that exposure to synthetic fabrics and estrogen can't be good for you. Hopefully, for one bridesmaid, beet juice proves to be equally nontoxic.

Nina M. was selected as one of four bridesmaids in the small-town wedding of a high school friend. It was the beginning of summer, and The Bride and her maids were still pasty from a winter of sun deprivation. All but one of them, that is. Bridesmaid number three showed up for the big event with a beautiful tanning booth skin tone, about twenty shades darker than the rest of the bridal party and only a moderately different hue than that of a chocolate fountain. On the day before the wedding, The Bride decided that everyone's skin must be made to coordinate, and that her dress should be the only blindingly white wedding accessory.

As Nina told it, the operative word was *glow*.

There were no tanning beds in the tiny town, but just down the country road from The Bride's house, a spray-on-tan outlet had recently opened. It was located in the back of a giant warehouse that was home to some sort of oil field operation. On the day of their spray, the women pulled their cars in among the big rigs and pickup trucks with no small amount of trepidation. Nina was fairly sure the sign advertising the salon was a joke, a way to lure hapless women off the road and get them to strip while construction workers watched through a peephole. With fear in their hearts, the bridal party made their way past grease-stained men taking smoke breaks, and prayed that the multiple vats of combustible petroleum products had nothing to do with the mystery substance in which they were soon to be doused.

"I was terrified," said Nina, who had never heard of spray-on tanning before that day. "And The Bride was basically using us as guinea pigs."

The women entered a tiny office and were shown an instructional video explaining that the tanning liquid was made of beet juice. The friendly female owner then demonstrated a series of moves they would be required to make inside the spraying booth, taking them through their paces like a slow-motion aerobics class. First they were to stand—butt naked—staring at the spray nozzles head on, their arms at their sides. After each hiss of the tanning spray, a red light would flash, signaling that the women should change positions. They had to do quarter turns, with one arm raised and the other lowered. They had to separate their legs so their inner thighs would be exposed, then turn to douse their sides and back. The owner stressed that their palms should always be positioned away from the nozzles, and warned that it would feel a little funny when they got a face full of beet juice.

"It's like you're in the video for 'Walk Like an Egyptian,'" Nina said, referencing a Bangles tune that has had no place anywhere near a wedding since 1988.

None of the bridesmaids wanted to be the first in the chamber, but The Bride refused to lead the charge. If anyone was going to be blinded, burned, or drowned in beet juice, it was not going to be her. Eventually, she ordered her younger sister to take the plunge. Youth before beauty, they say. After what felt like hours, the teenager emerged and the women inspected her for signs of streaks or post-traumatic stress. She appeared to be uniformly tanned and relatively unscathed, so bridesmaid number two took her turn.

Nina was still nervous, convinced that the machine would malfunction while she was inside, choking her slowly with a thickening mist of orange dye. She stripped down to her birthday suit, rubbed another mystery liquid on her fingernails to prevent them from staining, and took a deep breath.

"I was terrified I was going to come out looking like some streaky orange monster," she said.

Inside the booth things went relatively smoothly. She remembered to turn when the red light flashed and only momentarily felt like she had been lured into a B horror flick or government-sponsored chemical experiment. Finally, with all three bridesmaids a pleasant shade of peach, The Bride at last took her turn, satisfied that nothing could go wrong.

The next morning, Nina got in the shower early to get ready for the wedding and noticed that the water running down the drain was a deep shade of brown. She thought the city's water supply had been contaminated until she realized that the residue from her tan was being rinsed away.

The Bride, meanwhile, made the same discovery in a more traumatizing way. In the wedding photographs, large beet-colored stains were visible on the sides of her dress.

BIG M.A.C. ATTACK

Orange is still a better color to be seeing on your wedding day than red. Giselle W.'s bridal party started to crumble along with The Bride's nerves as the group got their hair and makeup done on the morning of the wedding. The

Bride, a friend of Giselle's from college, had "pre-approved" the two-time bridesmaid's hairstyle, a dramatic upsweep modeled on the one worn by Julia Roberts when she won her Oscar for *Erin Brockovich*. But when Giselle's hair was finished, The Bride decided it looked similar to her own and ordered her to have it redone.

His ego clearly damaged, the hairdresser reassembled Giselle's hair into a less fetching updo, adding to his already hefty fee of ninety-five dollars, and the wedding party headed for the mall to get their faces painted before the ceremony. To save time and the cost of having a makeup artist make a house call, each of them was booked at a different department store kiosk.

"So I was at M.A.C., one was at Christian Dior—we were all at different places," Giselle said. "And The Bride sort of floated from one to the next, checking up on us, because she was having hers done later at the hotel."

The bridal party was decked out in red velvet, a material usually reserved for vampire costumes or the curtains in a brothel. It was an October wedding, so the makeup artists began applying rich, earthy tones to complement the autumn theme.

Giselle had a shadow of dark red brushed on her eyelids, and another bridesmaid, Penny, wore deep red lipstick. When the girls' looks were complete, The Bride decided she did not approve.

"She came over and she said, 'Giselle, you can't have red eyes, and, Penny, your lipstick is too dark,' so we all went back and had our makeup redone."

The second time around, the wise young bridesmaids offered up their chosen lipsticks and eye shadows for approval *before* they were applied. Penny's new lipstick was given the green light, and she returned to her station for round two. Once her second makeover was done, The Bride suddenly appeared, rushing to the bridesmaid's side and saying, "No, no, I changed my mind. Change it again."

Each of the four bridesmaids had their cosmetics reapplied three times in slightly different shades, the makeup artists losing patience and silently reappraising their fifty-dollar flat rate, and *still* The Bride rejected the final product. Finally, Giselle said, Penny snapped and asked what the hell was going on.

The question was too much for the obviously frazzled bride. She screamed at her bridesmaids that it was her wedding and they would do as they were told, and they reciprocated her rage by detailing how awful their entire bridesmaid experience had been, from the boring shower to the blasé bachelorette. Soon, one of the other bridesmaids burst into tears, sending Deep Rose blush and Charcoal Rain mascara running all over her face, and The Bride sprinted off through the store. Her veil was already in place, and Giselle remembers seeing it trail behind her as she dashed into the purse section, her made-up maids in hot pursuit.

They cornered her near the Louis Vuittons and tried to calm her down—to no avail. Like a trapped fugitive going out in a blaze of gunfire, The Bride attacked, shooting off insults and saying she no longer wanted them in her wedding.

"This is the morning of. My hair is done, her veil is on, and we're standing in the middle of the mall yelling at each other," Giselle said. The Saturday shoppers stopped and stared, and the bridesmaids heard people whispering to one another, "Oh my God, they've been kicked out of a wedding."

As the cosmetics girls pointed and whispered and a bemused security guard looked on, The Bride repeated her decision that two of the four bridesmaids were no longer welcome at her wedding. The other two had bitten their tongues when their makeovers were undermined, and were spared The Bride's wrath.

Giselle and Penny left the mall and returned home, their precious hair and makeup still in place, wondering what the hell had just transpired.

Months later, Giselle found a photograph taken of the bridal party in the department store as they were getting their first round of makeup applied. They had gathered together for a quick snapshot, The Bride in the middle with her veil in place, their formal hairstyles illuminated by the glowing bulbs of the department store mirrors.

"We're sitting at the makeup counter together all lovey-dovey," Giselle said. "And five minutes later, drama unfolded."

7

THE BIG DAY

I was promised sex. Everybody said it. You'll be a bridesmaid, you'll get sex, you'll be fighting 'em off. But not so much as a tongue in sight.

—LYDIA, *Four Weddings and a Funeral*

There is exactly one photo of me from the wedding in which I was meant to be a bridesmaid. It is a beautiful scene, taken on the cobblestone terrace of an exclusive lakefront golf and country club. The table where I'm seated is surrounded by flowers, and in the background the grass rolls off into water and sunset like a lush green infinity pool.

I had thought about pulling the photographer aside when I arrived and asking her to avoid getting me in any of the official photographs, certain that the last thing The Bride would want floating on the periphery of her wedding memories was my grumpy face. I decided that was a bit melodramatic, though, so instead I spent the evening with one eye trained on the photographer, careful not to position myself between her and The Bride, bridesmaids, or any other important relative or guest on whom she may have been training her lens. But in the end, she got one by me.

A couple of months after the wedding, another bridesmaid e-mailed me the happy couple's online photo album, and I spent two hours at work clicking my way through it, praying that I wouldn't be in any of the shots and wishing The Bride didn't look so damn good in all of them. I stopped only briefly on the one of me, in which I sit hunched over, my black dress a blight against the fresh summer scene. I have since tried to expel thoughts of the photo's content from my mind, along with all memories of regrettable hookups and the fact that I wore overalls past the age of twenty. In the picture, I look like an angel of doom, an evil apparition sent to harvest the souls of unsuspecting wedding guests as they nibbled their shrimp from paper napkins—the Grim Reaper of Romanticism. I am sitting with my boyfriend and a bridesmaid, resplendent in her green silk dress, a cigarette in one of my hands and a drink in front of me, my mouth open in what appears to be mid-slur. I'm pretty sure it was the exact moment I was offering them money to let me go home.

I doubt the photo made it into the real album—unless they had a bloopers page—and in the long run I am proud of the fact that ultimately I did minimal damage to my former friend's wedding day. Let's face it, if I had succeeded in serving my full term as bridesmaid, I'd have giggled during the vows and almost certainly made an off-color remark during the bridesmaid speech. Although, she'd told me from the beginning there was no way I was getting my hands on a microphone. Who knows how many bridal party poses I would have tarnished with my half-closed eyes or haphazardly shaved legs? In the end, I ruined only one photograph at her wedding. Other women, I would like to point out, have done way more damage.

FOR BETTER OR FOR MUCH, MUCH WORSE

Sherri L. was posing for one last photograph with the bridal party when she left an indelible mark on her friend's wedding day. They were in the bridal room of the synagogue waiting to do the processional when the photographer declared he wanted one more premarital shot. There was a chaise lounge in the corner, and he directed The Bride to recline on it with her dress and her bridesmaids arrayed at her side. A sort of Last Supper for the Single Girl. As the other women perched awkwardly on the edge of the furniture or crouched low in the foreground, Sherri was told to position herself behind the chair, crammed between it and the wall and hidden among layers of puffy white fabric.

"I kneeled down and I don't know what I did, but I sat on her veil," the five-timer remembered.

Somehow she became tangled in the long piece of gauzy material and caused it to rip out of the headpiece that attached to The Bride's hair. The netting was too fine to repair and The Bride ended up walking down the aisle with a large hole running down the back of her veil and an even larger tear in the fabric of her mental health.

"She was distraught," Sherri said. "It was awful. I felt so bad."

There are a million tiny things that can go wrong with any wedding and in the organized chaos of bringing together a church full of tradition, tulle, personalities, and perfectionists. Every participant runs the risk of screwing up her individual role, but the bridesmaids face the additional pressure of having to move en masse on the big day, pulling off their duties in tandem like so many Russian synchronized swimmers, minus the nose plugs and testosterone-induced facial hair. And if bridesmaids think their aesthetic calisthenics during the engagement period are grueling, the day of the ceremony is like an obstacle course, which they must execute perfectly or risk sullying their friend's dream day.

Fiona H. had missed the rehearsal for her sister's wedding when she got stuck in traffic, and was unprepared for the elaborate Catholic service that had been organized to satisfy the wishes of the groom's family. The sisters had not grown up religious, and did not know their way around a church, so Fiona was told to simply follow her sister through each part of the service, straightening her train and taking whatever was handed to her. Everything was going alright until the couple headed up to light the unity candle halfway through the ceremony. Fiona missed her cue and stumbled, dropping the train and almost causing her sister to trip, and loudly whispered, "Shit," as she recovered.

"No," said the priest. "It's Holy Shit."

The Bride laughed at the time, as did the first few pews of guests who had heard the exchange, but the new couple's extended family was less than impressed when they discovered that the wedding video had recorded the obscenity for posterity.

At Lauren B.'s wedding, one of her attendants realized immediately before the ceremony that she had forgotten to bring her bouquet. Another quick-thinking bridesmaid came to her rescue by taking a few stems from each of the young flower girls' bouquets and fashioning them into an ad hoc bunch for the bridesmaid.

"Well, the little flower girls didn't appreciate it and their mothers certainly didn't appreciate it," Lauren said. "She was nearly shot."

The music had begun and the groomsmen had already taken their positions at the front of the synagogue, but when the women saw their daughters' bouquets being pillaged, they rushed from the pews and started berating the bridesmaids, screaming at them in full earshot of the congregation for having the gall to disrupt their little girls' finest moment.

"They started screaming, 'No, you may not take them,' and 'Are you insane trying to take a flower from a child?'" Lauren said. "So one of my bridesmaids walked without flowers." It appears that "something borrowed" refers only to the money needed to pay for the reception.

Holding up the processional while trying to rob a small child is only a minor inconvenience compared with the drama that can ensue if a bridesmaid gets too caught up in the moment.

Denise T. was in a wedding where one bridesmaid was paired with the groom's best man for the walk down the aisle, and the maid felt that their little stroll was leading somewhere other than just the reception.

"I guess everyone just gets overcome with emotion during weddings," Denise said. "And going through the motions with this guy convinced her that they were having some sort of connection."

The bridesmaid in question had a boyfriend of six years whom she'd left at home, and the best man had attended the wedding with his wife. Their son was the ring bearer. She was nonetheless so sure they had experienced a romantic vibe during the ceremony—a belief pickled in white wine as the evening wore on—that she cornered the best man after dinner and propositioned him.

"He was like, 'Listen, I have a wife and that's my kid,'" recounted Denise, who watched in dismay with The Bride as the scene unfolded. "She was like, 'It'll be fine. Come on.'"

Shot down, dead drunk, and utterly humiliated, the bridesmaid screamed nonsense at the other members of the wedding party, including The Bride's father. After being asked to leave the reception, she was kicked out of the hotel where it was being held for being unruly in the halls, and was eventually placed in a cab and sent packing.

"The Bride was embarrassed because the girl had just thrown herself at her husband's married friend," Denise said. "She was a bit annoyed, but I think she just felt bad for her."

At the brunch the next day, the disgraced bridesmaid hid inside while the object of her Wedding Goggles ate breakfast with his wife and the other guests on the terrace. "She wouldn't say anything to anyone, she was so embarrassed," Denise said. "Then she jumped in a cab to the airport and went back home."

TO HAVE AND TO HOLD IN

Being caught up in the romance of a wedding is a bridesmaid's occupational hazard. You are there, after all, to celebrate the fact that the bride has found the man of her dreams, when perhaps you have not. But there are more humiliating elements of a girl's character than desperation that can be exposed during a ceremony.

Amy O. attended a wedding where a bridesmaid's worst fears were realized as her best assets were exposed. The dress she was wearing had been accidentally delivered a size too small, but The Bride told her there was no time to get a new one and assured her that they would make it fit—or else.

On the day of the ceremony, the other bridesmaids squeezed her into the strapless gown, two of them holding the panels together while a third zipped it up like some sort of fleshy piece of periwinkle blue luggage.

"Halfway through the ceremony, the couple was in the middle of their vows and the zipper just popped," Amy remembered. "It wasn't boned or anything, so the dress just flopped down."

Luckily, the bridesmaid was wearing a strapless bra and had a very large bouquet of flowers that she immediately lifted in front of her chest. She stood there, half naked, as the couple continued their vows unaware that they were no longer the most interesting pair at the altar.

Another bridesmaid tried to lift the woman's dress back up, but she couldn't hold it in place with one hand without dropping her own bouquet, an act she must have decided would be too much of a disruption. Ironically, being a good bridesmaid often requires women to leave their humanity at home and their hands firmly at their sides.

"Of course it's already a big scene because there's a girl standing on the platform with her tits hanging out," Amy said. "Nobody's really listening to the bride and groom anymore. And they're wondering why everyone's hysterical with laughter and all the bridesmaids are bright red."

As the ceremony came to an end, two other bridesmaids lifted the disgraced girl's dress up and held it in place as they marched her out of the church.

"They safety-pinned her into the dress for the dinner because she had to make a speech," Amy said. "She didn't stay for the dance, though—she was too mortified."

Think about the celebrities you have seen on the pages of magazines in red carpet Don'ts or blunders. Their outfits are baggy or way too tight, their hair looks terrible, or they accidentally flash a shot of their crotch at the paparazzi and around the world. And these people travel with stylists, publicists, and bodyguards to ensure that nothing goes wrong during their public outings. So what chance does a bridesmaid stand of pulling it all off gracefully?

For her friend's nuptials, Emily R. was wearing a pair of heels that matched her champagne-colored bridesmaid dress and made her feet feel like they were slowly being gnawed from her body by tiny razor-toothed animals.

"They really, really hurt," said the three-time bridesmaid. "So in the middle of the ceremony, because my dress was floor-length, I took them off and stood in my bare feet."

The church full of flowers may have masked the odor of the bridesmaid's sweaty tootsies, but at the end of the ceremony, Emily suddenly realized she would have to put the shoes back on before she could walk back down the aisle. She began moving her feet around inside the train of her dress, desperately trying to locate the sandals, shuffling and swaying like a drunken uncle on the dance floor. As the rest of the bridal party stood calmly, trying not to react to Emily's contortionist vibrating, she ignored the "I dos" and the "You may kiss the bride" and focused on her slingbacks.

"I had flicked them sort of behind me, and they were wrapped in the back of my dress," she said.

There is something about weddings that shuts down the logical part of every woman's brain, so poor Emily did not realize that she could just as easily have walked out of the church barefoot, the way organized religion intended her to be. Instead, she stood there convulsing in her efforts to cram her feet into the shoes.

Like the brides themselves, wedding attendants can easily fall prey to nerves, cold feet, and the peculiar psychological ailments that are brought on by wedding ceremonies. The fear of looking bad—or, worse, stupid—in a bridesmaid dress is enough to drive a lot of women to extreme behavior. Many attendants join the gym and put themselves through strict wedding-ready diets to ensure that if the dress looks awful, it is the garment's fault and not their figure's. Toilet paper falsies, double-sided tape, and grim determination are all employed for maximum effect. And some simply stop eating altogether.

This was the case in one elaborate wedding that featured, among other things, a performer who was hired to be wheeled into the reception wearing the fruit table around her waist—a rolling, servile Carmen Miranda offering bunches of grapes and intricately carved kiwi fruit to the guests with her outstretched arms.

Before that could happen, though, the fourteen bridesmaids were determined to make a dazzling entrance in their own custom-designed gowns. Remember the bridal party that was told they could design their own dresses, setting off a battle of bitchiness? Well, they were also told to come ready at 8:00 A.M. even though the wedding didn't begin until 5:00 P.M., and most of them decided not to eat anything before the ceremony began, so as to look their anorexic best. By the time the bride and groom were ready to wed, they weren't the only ones feeling weak in the knees.

"Two of the bridesmaids fainted because they were hungry," said bridesmaid Jenny T. "The first girl went down before the glass was about to be shattered, and the other one went down just before the bride and groom were about to walk down the aisle when the ceremony was over."

The wedding had stretched on for forty-five minutes, and the bridesmaids were standing on a raised platform in a very hot room. After the first girl fainted, Jenny remembered a prolonged pause as the bridal party and guests tried to decide whether to call an ambulance or finish the vows.

"There's this girl next to me on the floor in convulsions and I'm just standing there with my bouquet trying to be calm, like everything's fine," she said. Being a Good Bridesmaid can be confusing, and unfortunately there is no etiquette book that specifies whether, in this situation, attendants are expected to check for a pulse or nudge their friend's body under the nearest pew with a delicately extended leg.

As Jenny waged an internal battle between being Good and doing CPR, people seated in the back started standing up to see what was going on. For about ten or fifteen seconds no one moved. Everyone just sort of stopped and stared at the unconscious young woman lying at The Bride's feet.

"Then two people picked her up, moved her off to the side, sat her in a chair, and the wedding just kept going," Jenny said. "It was literally about five minutes before the other one went down."

TO SNUB AND TO CHERISH

Being a bridesmaid wouldn't be so bad if we could all just lapse into unconsciousness and awake to find the whole thing over and done with. Unfortunately, the opportunities for disaster multiply as the day wears on, and the bridal party is kept alert with a steady stream of caffeine, stress, and peer pressure. The average wedding is now thirty-six consecutive hours of bridal mania, beginning with a rehearsal dinner and ending only after every family dysfunction has been exposed.

The presence of bridesmaids throughout all of this is actually about as necessary to the wedding ceremony as the bride's virginity.

Kimberly C. saw her efforts as a bridesmaid completely ignored on the day of the ceremony. The event was taking place in a northern Canadian resort town during shad fly season, a two-week period when the large, mouthless insects descend on the region like bulimics in a Burger King bathroom.

"They live for twenty-four hours, mate, and die," she said. "When they die they pile up and accumulate to inches of crunchy dead shad flies."

Because no one had considered scheduling the wedding during one of the fifty weeks of the year when the entire town was not coated in carcasses, Kimberly spent the morning of her friend's wedding day the way she had always imagined it as a little girl: hosing away dead flies. Along with her sister, who was also in the wedding, Kimberly had already taken a week off from work to help with such glamorous prep. The bridesmaids had bought hundreds of candles for the outdoor party, decorated the hall with fake sunflowers, cooked the vegetarian entrée for the reception, called one another names as the stress level grew, and baked and decorated a cake when The Bride realized she had forgotten to order one. When it was time for the ceremony, Kimberly and her sister marched down the outdoor aisle as the shad flies swarmed around them, a grotesque challenge of *Fear Factor* proportions.

"You had to walk with your mouth closed and hands over your eyes," Kimberly said of the bugs. To make matters worse the aisle ran over a grassy hill, and her strappy sandals sank into the ground with each step. "So I looked like I had some sort of jerky palsy."

After Kimberly and her sister swallowed their pride, the cost of their duties, and at least four shad flies each, The Bride forgot to mention them during the wedding party introductions. "We cried," she said.

Even in Victorian times, bridesmaids were largely overlooked during the ceremonies themselves. According to Ann Monsarrat, author of *And the Bride Wore . . . The Story of the White Wedding*, the nineteenth-century bridesmaid's most cumbersome job was holding the bride's gloves while she exchanged rings with her man.

In other parts of the world, bridesmaids have historically been stuck with equally unglamorous and unrewarding roles. At Belgian weddings in the early twentieth century, bridesmaids collected money from the guests and threw the coins to the poor people gathered outside, cementing a reputation of generosity for the new couple. In ancient Asia, bridesmaids would stand upon the threshold of the bride's house and refuse to let the hopeful groom enter until they were sure he had earned her hand, pegging him with rice balls as he bribed them with gifts.

Nowadays, most attendant attacks are reserved for one another, with any goodwill evaporating as they throw most of their own coin into the wedding preparations.

Geena R. was asked to be Maid of Honor by her older sister, despite the fact that the two women were not particularly close. On the day of the wedding, after months of preparations, the other women in the party—close friends of The Bride—decided to pull rank and reassign Geena's Big Day tasks.

"It was just this big melee. I thought they were going to tear out each other's hair." She shuddered.

One of The Bride's friends appointed herself MOH and gave the other two subsidiary roles, dividing up Geena's duties like the estate of a hated parent. Geena did not stand next to her sister during the ceremony, or sign the license as a witness, or deliver the speech she had written.

"I pretty much just sat at the head table by myself," she said. "At that point, I was only still there because I had the dress."

If she had a rice ball, she would not have thrown it at the groom.

TO DISHONOR AND OBEY

To prevent any last-minute awkwardness or black-tie coups d'état, weddings are usually as choreographed, scripted, and decidedly unnatural as Tom Cruise in a May-December romance.

For her friend's wedding, Leah F. and her fellow brides-maids received an e-mail a full month in advance outlining explicit instructions for the wedding day itinerary and their individual assignments. One woman was instructed to hang back at the church after the ceremony to make sure everyone got in the right car, and another was told to stay with The Bride at all times to make sure nobody got lipstick on her cheek or a drink near her dress. It is possible, Leah acknowledged, that The Bride actually wanted this friend to throw herself into the path of incoming red wine, sacrificing life and limb just like Kevin Costner does for Whitney Houston in *The Bodyguard*, or as Whitney Houston is rumored to do for crack cocaine in real life.

"She actually did end up getting orange juice spilled on her dress," Leah said. "And we're a bit suspicious that it might have been on purpose."

The paranoid bride probably invited such hostility by assigning her attendants a litany of ridiculous duties and then deciding she didn't trust them to follow through. There is nothing worse than being second-guessed all day long by the woman who forced you to wear lavender eye shadow so it would match her bouquet. When Leah's bride entered the reception at the fancy Ritz hotel, she spent an hour moving place cards around because she wasn't happy with how the bridesmaids had done it. She'd also made them all take dance classes so they would look good on the floor beside her, and she got angry if any of the bridesmaids left the reception without permission.

According to Leah, "Somebody went to the bathroom during the father-daughter dance, and she freaked." Apparently, bridesmaids not only require a strong sense of duty, but also superhuman bladder control.

Being trapped inside the dream day of a female friend can be scary for a lot of women, especially if there's a ban on the bathroom or a line for the bar. Having to dance with a creepy uncle or absorb a spill with your chest is nothing, however, compared to the task that Wendy H. was handed at one of her friends' weddings.

It was the year she was a bridesmaid seven times, so you'd think she would have seen it all, but there was no way to prepare for this one. The Bride was a high school friend and also a Mormon. Wendy was not, and the attendant discovered that she would not actually be allowed to "attend" the ceremony, as it were.

The invitations had specified that only Mormons were allowed in the temple for the vows, but everyone was welcome at the reception afterward. Unfortunately many of the guests—perhaps tired of analyzing the subtext of wedding invitations to establish who paid for what—had glossed over the fine print and come to the church expecting both a program and a pew. It was Wendy's job to enforce the No Sinners clause.

"They would come up, and you kind of knew they weren't Mormon because they didn't know what any of the procedures were," Wendy noted. "I wasn't allowed even inside the doors; I was on the church steps. So I was standing out there with this nice lady from the church and a guest list of who was Mormon and who wasn't."

As politely as possible, Wendy would point out the "Mormons Only" line on the wedding invitations and apologize profusely before sending guests in the direction of the reception hall, which gracefully admitted those likely to burn in Hell. Still, her main purpose was not merely to restrict entry to followers of the Latter-Day Saints—that would be too meek a challenge for a nonbeliever such as she. No, Wendy was also charged with preventing the incursion of The Bride's Estranged Father, who had not been invited to either portion of the festivities.

"He'd been excommunicated for divorcing her mother," Wendy explained. "He did show up at the reception but he never went by the church." Thank God.

IN SICKNESS AND IN FAKE SICKNESS

I felt sick throughout most of the wedding in which I was meant to be a bridesmaid. Dramatically demoted, I sat on the sidelines and flushed with fever whenever anyone looked in my direction, felt my heart skip as my friends joined The Bride in the hora, flinging each other around in joyful abandon, and wanted to throw up when the bridesmaid speech paid tribute to The Bride's ability to "stick with you through anything." As much as I envisioned dying of rejection and embarrassment, and knew our friendship had suffered a debilitating stroke, I always knew I would survive her day.

Caroline H. had her doubts on that score. She was a bridesmaid for the first and only time in a wedding held at a South American island resort. She and her fiancé, who was also in the wedding, decided to make a vacation out of it and set off for a week of sun, surf, and strutting their stuff across the sand for the couple's exotic nuptials. After just a few days in the beautiful country and perhaps one too many cocktails mixed with the local ice cubes, an intestinal parasite struck up a love affair with Caroline's insides. Soon, her romantic getaway and bridesmaid duties took a backseat to her relationship with the toilet in her hotel room, where she found herself trapped for hours at a time. As the wedding guests attended a "Welcome Party" at the resort, Caroline said good-bye to her lunch. As the bridal party digested their rehearsal dinner, Caroline vowed never to eat again.

"I was heaving my way through the bridesmaid luncheon, couldn't lie out in the sun, couldn't get in the pool, couldn't drink mimosas," she said forlornly. "They looked like they were having so much fun, and I hadn't eaten in three days." Caroline had, however, received a house call the day before from an island doctor who administered a four-hundred-dollar shot in the ass with what she now suspects were grossly expired antibiotics. "Just when I thought I was getting better," she said, "I started the second bottle of meds and got hit with another tornado in my gut."

Caroline worried that everyone would assume she had really just had too much to drink, but she could do little to dissuade them with her daily routine of puking and pouring with sweat.

To make matters even more painful, The Bride's grandmother—while outwardly concerned—seemed skeptical of Caroline's ability to "smile and look pretty" during the marriage ceremony. At one point, the drug-dishing doyenne even offered the ailing attendant a suppository from her personal stash.

On the day of the wedding, Caroline managed to stay upright without anything inserted up her bum and smiled during the brief ceremony even as her stomach churned. When the music began, though, and The Bride's brother asked her to dance, Caroline had to tango with the toilet instead. She lay there sprawled on the tile floor of her paradise hotel room, shivering, wearing a black hooded sweatshirt over her dress, and listening to the eight-hour party going on directly below her balcony, a sound drowned out only by her occasional cries of agony.

Halfway through the reception, the other wedding attendants were invited onstage to participate in a wedding ritual where single women pull charms out of a cake, with each one meant to symbolize the profession of their future husbands.

"I could just barely hear, 'We need the bridesmaids up here. All the bridesmaids please come up to the cake table!'" Caroline said. "And a little while later, 'Where's Caroline? Caroline! We need you at the cake table!'"

As her own insides were being yanked out of their moorings, Caroline's fiancé subbed in and drew her charm out of the cake on a long pink ribbon. The bauble, along with a Tiffany necklace that Caroline received as a bridesmaid gift despite her lack of participation, was all she had to show for the trip—except, she pointed out, "a lingering stomach problem."

Anyone who has experienced a bout of food poisoning knows that it is one of the most painful things a person can go through. You sit down for a nice meal or a quick roadside taco and the next thing you know, you wish you were dead. Being a reluctant bridesmaid is not so different an experience, minus the devastating cramps. Something that seems so natural and lovely, a wedding, soon has you on your knees begging for mercy.

Two Los Angeles bridesmaids escaped this fate by feigning an illness rather than let a boring wedding suck the life out of them, thus proudly adopting the title of Bad Bridesmaids rather than meekly accepting a night of bad dancing.

Brooke B. and Kelli F. had been asked to stand up for Barb, a girl they had met in their first year of college. They had hung out a bit, but after Barb transferred to another program on campus, the women did not hear from her until she called to announce her engagement and ask them to be bridesmaids.

After they said yes ("What else do you say?" explained Brooke), Barb informed them that her wedding would be held on Memorial Day weekend, just a few months away. Another mutual friend of theirs had been engaged for more than a year, and her wedding was also scheduled for that day, something the bridesmaids pointed out to Barb—to no avail. Borrowing a tired plotline from *The OC*, Barb had met her fiancé only six months before but would not negotiate on the date, even if it meant her bridesmaids would have to choose one wedding over another. They had been tricked into a game of Bridesmaid Bait and Switch, agreeing to their roles before the other bride had technically requested an RSVP.

To add insult to injury, The Bride informed the women that they were expected at the rehearsal promptly at 3:30 P.M., but that they were, unfortunately, not invited to the dinner afterward.

"'It's just family,'" Brooke recalled The Bride explaining. "But everyone else in the wedding is family, so basically everyone went to dinner except for Kelli and me."

The ceremony was being held an hour and a half away from the California town where Kelli and Brooke went to school, and they had no place to stay the night before the wedding, so they told The Bride they would just come down on Saturday and skip the rehearsal altogether. "How hard is it to walk down the aisle?" Brooke reasoned.

The Bride had no patience for this classic Bad Bridesmaid logic, and had other plans for her attendants. She wanted them to spend the night with her before the wedding, keeping her company in a luxurious hotel room that they would split three ways. Stunned but unwilling to say no because they believed Bad Bridesmaid karma would be visited upon them during their own weddings, the two women drove to the rehearsal site, participated in the run-through, and then went to a bar to drink alone while the rest of the family had dinner. The next morning, as they nursed their hangovers and growing resentment, The Bride informed them that she was moving immediately into the bridal suite and that they would promptly have to check out of the room they'd all shared the night before.

"There's three hours until the wedding, and we have nowhere to go," Brooke said. "We're like, what are we supposed to do, sit down on the floor in front of the bridal suite?"

Eventually, it was time for the wedding. The ceremony was mercifully short and attended by only about fifty guests. By 9:00 P.M. dinner had been served, the speeches spoken, and Kelli and Brooke were sitting at a table with The Bride's teenage brother, bored out of their minds.

"So I look over at Kelli and say, 'I have to get out of here,'" Brooke remembered. "'How long do you think it would take to get to Amy's wedding?'"

Kelli looked at her friend with a completely straight face and replied in a loud voice, "Oh my God, I think my face is swelling."

The twenty-six-year-old actually suffers from a condition called angiodoema, which is basically a severe allergic reaction to everything from dust to spider bites. It is also, conveniently enough, the most perfect "out" imaginable.

"So I go, 'Oh my God, it is,'" said Brooke, her voice filled with mock concern. "'We're going to have to go home and get your medicine!'"

With that, Kelli ran to the hotel valet and picked up her car, while Brooke informed The Bride of the impending fake medical emergency.

"We got in the car and drove to the other wedding and stayed there for the rest of the night," Brooke said. "It was so fun."

The next day, the women received an e-mail from The Bride. She did not ask about Kelli's condition or thank them for their help with her day. She told them that the cost of their valet parking had been charged to her room and that they owed her forty-two dollars.

"I don't even think she really cared that we left. We had served our purpose," said Brooke. "And I haven't heard from her since."

8

THE HONEYMOON'S OVER

Carrie: How do you tell somebody you don't want to be a part of their wedding?

Miranda: If I knew that, I wouldn't be in charge of the guest book.

—*Sex and the City*

It is sad to admit that a wedding ended one of the great love affairs of my life. I had prized my friendship with The Bride, as different as we were, and had even joked in a toast at her shower that she was cheating on me with her groom-to-be. Her previous boyfriends had brought us closer, I laughed, giving us something to complain about and discuss over drinks, and I was jealous that she had finally found someone who would make her girlfriends take second place.

In the end though, it was her wedding—not her man— that would put an end to our friendship.

Since her beautiful day, which I observed from the back row, we have seen each other only at dinner parties held by mutual friends. I was demoted from her bridal party, and we slipped from each other's lives.

It may seem silly, but weddings have been shown to create more stress than most other experiences in a person's life, from job interviews to army interrogations. No one will argue that planning a large-scale event with such lasting importance can breed sleepless nights for the bride and groom and their respective families. Few people acknowledge, though, the brunt of the stress borne by bridesmaids.

In 2001, a doctoral student at Ohio State University named Montenique Finney wanted to determine whether having a friend around during a stressful situation made things better or worse, and she selected forty college-aged women to act as her guinea pigs. To get their blood boiling, Finney had them prepare a two-minute speech on a hypothetical situation. She could have chosen war or famine, politics or pop culture—topics most likely to get someone good and riled up. Instead, she had the women pretend they were bridesmaids—Maids of Honor, in fact—and that their dresses had been delivered one week before the wedding with major design flaws.

Each of the women was asked to write down what she would say to the store manager when she learned of this fashion disaster, and then perform her make-believe rant for the researcher in a role-playing exercise. Finney must have been a wedding attendant herself at one point, because this scenario could only have been dreamed up by a former Bad Bridesmaid with a wicked sense of humor.

Finney took blood samples to establish her subjects' cholesterol levels and found that all of the women experienced a dramatic rise in stress as they got more and more worked up delivering their angry dress diatribes. And here's where it gets interesting: half of the test subjects also had a friend standing at their side as they reamed out the imaginary store clerk. Those women had cholesterol levels *three times* as high as those who ranted alone.

Finney concluded that, contrary to popular belief, friends do not help you calm down, and advised women to leave their girlfriends at home when entering a stressful situation—words of wisdom that could save generations of wedding attendants from dangerous tours of duty.

Because it's not Bad Bridesmaids who cause the problems—it's the stress. It's been scientifically proven.

CASE DISMISSED

Sadly, I am neither the first nor the last woman to be dismissed from a friend's bridal party. Some brides decide that their attendants have been consistently unhelpful and do not deserve a front-row seat, giving them their walking papers after prolonged deliberation. Others experience a blowout (and not the hundred-dollar kind) over an outfit hated or obligation unmet. The weddings go on, but the friendship is rarely salvaged.

Keltie H. was kicked out of the wedding of one of her best and oldest friends, a woman she now considers dead to her. There were four bridesmaids, all of whom had hung out with The Bride and one another since high school, tight for more than ten years. Keltie and another bridesmaid, Tia, were still in school when the engagement took place, and did not have the money or time to throw themselves into the wedding prep with abandon. By the time January rolled around, just halfway through the yearlong engagement, the two Bad Bridesmaids had already said no to several excursions and shown up late for a dress shopping trip, having driven to The Bride's hometown after class on a Friday.

The Bride was fed up.

"She said, 'You guys don't care about my wedding. Your number one priority is school,'" Keltie remembered. "And I said, 'Yes, it is.'"

The Bride was not willing to take a backseat to higher education, so she kicked the two bridesmaids to the curb. They were furious, and amazed when two of the other bridesmaids sided with The Bride and stopped talking to them as well.

After ten years of friendship and just six months of lackluster bridesmaiding, the women did not even get an invitation to the wedding. They sent The Bride a dozen roses on the day of the ceremony and a card that said, "Hope you're having a great day." What color of roses denotes sarcasm, I wonder?

Keltie has now been a bridesmaid four times in total, and never had a problem with any other bride, but she has not spoken to the woman who gave her the boot—or the other bridesmaids—since the days after her dismissal.

"I can't forgive someone who did that to me. It's brutal. Everyone knows we're in your wedding party and now everyone knows we're not. It is a public embarrassment," she said. "To me that's the end of the friendship."

Remember Giselle, who was kicked out of her friend's wedding on the morning of the ceremony? She and another bridesmaid drove home in a state of shock, thinking, "Is this really happening?"

Both women were upset—they had just been screamed at in a crowded mall after refusing to have their makeup redone for a fourth time—but neither was yet willing to accept that such a petty argument spelled the end of their involvement in their friend's wedding. With time still remaining before The Bride walked down the aisle, they called her cell phone and asked if she was ready to change her mind. Despite the nasty words, and the public humiliation, Giselle said both women were willing to stand at The Bride's side throughout her wedding, rather than create more controversy in absentia. The Bride was not so understanding, and instead of apologizing to her bridesmaids, she hung up on them.

After the initial shock wore off and Giselle had scrubbed all traces of costume makeup from her tearstained face, the ousted bridesmaid's sadness turned to anger. Her mother had thrown The Bride a shower, and their family had fêted her with gifts she was unlikely to return. Giselle had spent four hundred dollars alone on a full-length red velvet dress and matching opera-length gloves, which remain to this day wrapped in plastic in the dismissed bridesmaid's closet.

She estimated that her friend's wedding cost her more than a thousand dollars, and concluded that her investment should be paid back in full. Signing on to be a bridesmaid, she reasoned, is a contractual agreement where women consent to spend money on gifts, showers, and dresses in exchange for a walk-on role in the wedding. Not necessarily a fair trade, but a well-established barter of money for prestige. Giselle considered her friend in breach of contract, and she wasn't going to walk away without a fight.

She contacted a lawyer and asked if she was in a position to sue, and though the lawyer agreed that theoretically a contract had been violated, he told her it wasn't worth the hassle of a trip to court.

"He said I would be stuck in a legal battle for years 'Over what—a dress?'"

In retrospect, Giselle probably should have contacted a female lawyer more likely to have been a bridesmaid once herself—because anyone who's been in a wedding knows that a dress is never just a dress. With a crusading former wedding attendant on her side, imagine the news coverage of the precedent-setting case:

JURY OUT IN BRIDESMAID V. BRIDE

WEDDING INDUSTRY SUFFERS MAJOR
THIRD-QUARTER LOSS AS ENGAGED COUPLES
ANXIOUSLY AWAIT COURT RULING

Always the bridesmaid? That could mean a huge payoff for some women, as a court deliberates on the responsibilities of brides toward their disgruntled former wedding attendants.

A jury of seven men and five women (three of whom are former bridesmaids) has been sequestered since yesterday afternoon, tasked with deciding whether ousted bridesmaids deserve financial compensation for their wedding-related duties. In anticipation of the controversial ruling, a group of women in hideous pastel-colored dresses has gathered in front of the courthouse, threatening to riot if the court rules in favor of brides. The case, which stretched on over months like a typical engagement period and called more than 200 witnesses, saw a cranberry bridesmaid dress entered as evidence under Exhibit A, for *atrocious*.

Security presence throughout the city has been beefed up in anticipation of the ruling, and weddings throughout the country have reached an all-time low as bridesmaids withhold their services in solidarity with the plaintiff. Vera Wang could not be reached for comment.

Instead, Giselle is just another girl who got slapped with the Bridal Backhand, destined to have jokes made at her expense for eternity. Her dramatic expulsion has become a running comedy routine in her family, who enjoy teasing her for failing to be Good Bridesmaid material. Whenever she is asked to stand up for a friend (and she has been twice since then) her parents question the bride to make sure she knows what sort of attendant she's getting.

"Are you sure you want to have Giselle in the wedding?" they ask innocently. "Do you know what happened last time?"

REPEAT OFFENDERS

There is no equation that can calculate a woman's likelihood of being a bridesmaid, but if you take the number of your female friends (X) divided by a variable of closeness (Y), subtracting those you will lose to international moves or the Church of Scientology (Z), and multiply by

Murphy's Law, you may have a rough estimate of how many times you will have to go through it.

Some women manage to avoid the role entirely, and I would hazard a guess that these people live longer, like pampered celebrities or the inhabitants of a tranquil Pacific island untouched by technology or war. They should be rounded up and studied, their pheromones extracted and speech patterns monitored so we can establish the root of their immunity and then make millions marketing a Bridesmaid Vaccine.

Other women are Chronic Bridesmaids, walking down the aisle twice a year from the time their first sorority sister pulls the trigger on a shotgun wedding until their fingers are raw from clapping politely and clawing for the bouquet.

The rest of us fall somewhere in between, participating in a handful of weddings during our late twenties and early thirties and then doing our best to erase the memories, chalking them up to a "phase," like same-sex kisses in college or wearing dresses over jeans.

But relying on the fact that our bridesmaid days are numbered—ending as our last friend ties the knot or settles for artificial insemination—overlooks our responsibility to bridesmaids of the future, who deserve to be saved like so many helpless seal pups. According to the Fairchild Bridal Bank, the Echo Boom—children of the Baby Boomers, who were born between 1979 and 2002—will soon move into the "engagement zone," that exciting period of their late twenties when diamonds start flying like buns in a food fight. This means that more than seventy-one million men and women will get hitched and require bridesmaids over the decades to come, an entire generation of women paralyzed by the duties of their friends' wedding preparations. Their careers will suffer, their sense of fashion will atrophy, and they will come to believe that lobster tail always tastes cold and rubbery. Before this sad day, when women are forced to spend an entire decade in bridesmaid-related meetings and men are left to wander the streets alone, we must learn how to say no when someone pops the question, or at least how to politely escape some of the more onerous tasks.

Madison V., who is thirty-one, has been a bridesmaid eight times since her early twenties, and said she has never contemplated saying no to any of her engaged friends.

"I never thought about saying no because it's never been an option. Well," she retracted, "I've thought about it, but the words have never left my lips."

Some women have a hard time turning down any offer (and we all know what to call them); others say yes because they have deluded themselves into thinking that it won't be so bad this time.

Summer J. has been a bridesmaid six times, and said it was exciting only twice, when she was young and the concept of weddings was romantic and new. Back then, the thought of a friend getting married was exotic, and came with a chance to dress up, make an emotional speech, and drain the open bar.

"Once you get to like twenty-nine, thirty, weddings are getting a bit old, and the whole thing's just a hassle," she said. "Every single time I'm asked to be a bridesmaid now, I think, 'Oh, god. People are buying gowns for their grade-eight grads now. So imagine what they expect for their wedding.'"

Summer wishes she had persuaded her friend The Bride to tone down those expectations during her engagement, because she is now carrying them into motherhood. Three months before giving birth to her first child, she called Summer to complain that no one had offered to organize a baby shower. This was because all of her former bridesmaids were still recovering from the nightmare of their wedding experience, during which they'd had to arrange and pay for various parties, showers, and events.

"She was so horrified that people would see that she didn't have a baby shower," Summer said. "It's all about what it looks like." And according to Summer, the two are not even particularly close since the wedding. "We're friends but not buddies," she said. "I don't think she would rely on me to take a bullet for her."

INSTANT BAD KARMA

There is one promise that is made to every bridesmaid to compensate for the particular humiliation she is forced to endure, whether it is having a baby blue tutu fitted to her hips or being asked to groove down the aisle to the beats of Jay-Z's "99 Problems," an idea that will surely surface sooner or later.

No, it is not the reassurance that you will one day be able to look back at the experience fondly, laughing at your outfit and remarking on how catchy that tune really was. We are expected to take comfort in the fact that we can inflict similar suffering on our own bridesmaids.

Revenge is a dish best served cold, and in the world of weddings, it comes with a side of frosty attendants. Complain about your bridesmaid duties, and another woman will undoubtedly point out that you can inflict the same thing as payback when *your* special day comes. The idea of exacting retribution on female friends is troubling on many levels, and we'd probably be better off just to stage a cage match at the altar and end the cycle of violence right there.

Some women profess more pure motivations for standing up beside a betrothed friend. When Faye S. got married, her friend was Super Bridesmaid, her utility belt well stocked with Advil, Pepto-Bismol, hairpins, tampons, and extra pantyhose. She threw parties and organized bands, kept the ring bearer on his Ritalin, and thawed out The Bride's cold feet. So when it was Faye's turn to be a bridesmaid in her friend's wedding, she felt she owed it to her to perform similarly, even though she lacked the genetic predisposition for creating bridal shower loot bags.

"I wanted to be as good a bridesmaid as she was," said Faye. "I just wasn't cut out for it."

Other women are motivated by neither revenge nor gratitude, but simply the pursuit of good karma. They are trying to score brownie points for their own weddings, among their family and friends and the larger powers-that-be.

Brooke B. and her friend Kelli F., who faked an illness to escape the reception of a bride they did not really like, were even warned by their parents, "Do not be in this wedding. She's not your friend."

The Bride was rude to them throughout the engagement period, and did not thank them for a shower they threw in her honor. When the wedding party gifts were handed out, the women watched as the groomsmen opened cuff links, silk ties, and cigars, and they were each handed a grocery bag filled with a single *Cosmopolitan* magazine, a lip gloss, and a package of facial wipes. Still, the women swallowed their pride and focused on how they would benefit when their own weddings came around.

Kelli was getting married the following year, and they decided that they had to cooperate as bridesmaids so she would have stories to leverage against her own attendants.

"We did it to protect ourselves," Brooke said. "But since then, all we did was talk shit about it. So that might cancel it out."

AS GOOD AS IT GETS

No one starts off as a Bad Bridesmaid. It's like an allergic reaction that develops with age, bred in a culture that has turned weddings into large-scale productions with no margin of error and has made a generation of women highly sensitive to ugly dresses and passive-aggressive bitchiness. Still, before our first time leading someone down the aisle, most women look forward to the opportunity to stand on the front lines, a roomful of people admiring their pastel posse, a place of honor reserved at the head table, and their legacy ensured in the wedding photo album and on the commemorative DVD.

Giselle W., who considered suing her former friend after being dismissed from a wedding party, still remembers how excited she was when she was first asked to be a bridesmaid, at age twelve. "I was one of fifteen bridesmaids for my cousin, and I was so excited," she said. "I felt like I was royalty."

So why is it that so many bridesmaids end up feeling less like princesses and more like prisoners of war? No one wants to be the one disappointing element of a perfect wedding, and most women facing bridal party pressure do their best to at least play along, even if they don't like the rules.

There seems to be no rhyme or reason for women becoming the Bad Bridesmaids of the world, loudly questioning the need for another shower or laughing hysterically when the ceremonial dove flies into an electrical line. Some women butt their beautiful heads with sisters and best friends, others with distant acquaintances or former colleagues. A few bridal disasters are born of lingering resentment, others explode out of a single slight or sequence of events. All of the brides who make their attendants feel Bad do have one thing in common, though: they see their bridesmaids as wedding accessories instead of friends, if only for a moment.

Paula J., a woman who has been a bridesmaid six times with varying levels of posttraumatic stress, said the best brides are the ones who are less concerned with the details.

"They don't care if your shoes all match, they don't care if your speech is two minutes or ten minutes, they don't care what time you get there," she said. Being asked to be a bridesmaid in those cases, Paula remembers, is about having fun together and celebrating something bigger than both of you, and the resulting euphoria brings out the best in even the worst Former Bridesmaids. "You actually want to do things for them then," she said. "You think it would actually be nice to buy her a drink, or whatever, because you're doing things on your own initiative and not because she told you to do it."

Another woman battled through being Bad by refusing to back down to her friend's demands, and pointing out when The Bride was being unreasonable, advice she viewed as her duty as a lifelong friend.

"I wouldn't stand up for her if I didn't support her and if I didn't believe she was marrying a really nice guy who was crazy about her," said Madison K. "We've been friends since the fifth grade. If I can't tell her that her ideas totally suck, and use those words, our friendship wouldn't have lasted that long."

Barbara M. has been a bridesmaid more than fifteen times, beginning with a sorority sister bride in 1995. Since then, she has stood up for friends, sisters, cousins, and in-laws, and her only complaint has been the quality of the dresses, one of which was robin's egg blue and another that had a "big old bow" stapled to the butt.

Besides those unfortunate clothing choices, she said all of her bridesmaid experiences have been good ones, and have taken her to such beautiful destinations as Aspen, Belize, and the Cayman Islands.

"Nothing's gone wrong," she said. "I don't know why, because you always hear horror stories."

Barbara cannot explain how she has managed to escape unscathed when so many women have lost friends and financial independence as a result of just one wedding. The saying "Thrice a bridesmaid, never a bride" was born of the belief that bridesmaids absorbed evil curses directed at the bride during weddings, and would eventually be damaged beyond repair. If this is true, maybe Barbara has been permanently damaged by her bridesmaid duties, suffering early-onset dementia that prevents her from recalling the traumatic incidents of her past. She prefers to believe that her happy experiences are credited to the fact that she has no "bridezilla" friends, and that all of the women she stood up for were unusually low maintenance. With fifteen weddings, though, she has probably lost one whole year of her life attending showers, bachelorettes, and loan-approval meetings at her local bank branch. So has she ever considered saying no—not out of fear but simply to avoid the cost and time commitments?

"No. Not ever an option," she protests innocently. "Have people done that?"

THE MOURNING AFTER

Sarah G. did not say no when she was asked to be a bridesmaid for a woman she and her boyfriend met on vacation in Mexico. Recall that she endured awkward showers knowing no one, bought an expensive dress, and even let the groom-to-be crash at her new house before the whole ordeal was over.

She drove home from that wedding, threw her ugly dress directly in the garbage, and sat on the couch like a zombie until dawn, when her parents woke up and asked her what was wrong.

"I just had the worst night of my life," she remembers telling them.

She spent more than $1,000 on the wedding, including $200 on the dress, $150 for the bachelorette, $100 for the shower gift, and $150 for the wedding gift. In retrospect, she realizes she should have said no, explaining that she and her boyfriend had just bought a house and could not afford—mentally or financially—to be involved.

Instead, after the dust cleared, Sarah and her boyfriend broke up and sold their house. The couple who had put so much strain on their relationship divorced less than a year after their wedding, and Sarah lost touch with The Bride until recently.

Suddenly the woman began calling her again, trying to rekindle the friendship, and sending Sarah into panic mode. The battered bridesmaid admits she is now avoiding

The Bride, not because of the past, but because of what could happen in the future.

"What if she gets married again?" Sarah asked. "I can't be anywhere near that."

If Sarah's is not enough of a cautionary tale, listen to the experts. Wedding planner and bridal boutique owner Deb McCoy thinks nuptial preparations have gotten so out of control that it's hard to see what really matters.

"We have to get back to the basic perception of the wedding as a family and friend affair, where the bride and groom take their guests into consideration before they take themselves into consideration," she said. "If you do that, people will walk out saying, 'Wow, what a wonderful party.'"

Then again, not everyone is convinced this can happen. Cele Otnes, author of *Cinderella Dreams: The Allure of the Lavish Wedding*, says it's unlikely that women will walk away from having the wedding of their dreams, no matter what the repercussions on their real-life relationships. There were times in history, she said, when weddings became less elaborate for a period, going "back into the parlor," so to speak. This happened, she pointed out, only when society was experiencing widespread strife, like an economic downturn or maybe an international conflict.

"I don't know what would make it go down unless we go into a world war," she said. "There are just too many players involved."

Deciding between nuclear annihilation and a bad bridesmaid dress will be a tough call for a lot of women, but Otnes does not see a third option. Asking for weddings to become less manic affairs is like wishing tuition fees would drop to triple digits—it's just not going to happen.

"There are sometimes these little pockets of resistance, where women advocate for wearing their mother's wedding dress," she said. "I think we may have passed the point of no return, and it would take an awful lot to go back."

Judith Martin, author of the syndicated "Miss Manners" column, receives so many letters from bridesmaids asking her about their recourse that she joked about founding a "labor union for bridesmaids to ensure them decent working conditions, proper uniforms and limited financial liability."

This is actually not a bad idea. Brides get prenups, hotels get damage deposits, and even the mentally ill get some nice soothing medication. Yes, bridesmaids get the earrings or the bracelet, and they're lovely—thank you. But while the bride and groom head off on their honeymoon (paid for, no doubt, through a bridesmaid-organized shower), the bridesmaids go back to being slightly less financially secure versions of themselves, with one more outfit they won't wear and the beginnings of a serious alcohol-dependency problem.

We are not asking for a lot in exchange, just a little respect. We want more than a toast from the groom's less attractive brother: we want to stop being the whipping girls of weddings and the butt of jokes penned by Hollywood screenwriters who use bridesmaids as shorthand for desperate spinster or psycho singleton.

When a wedding is complete, few people sit back and say, "She made a beautiful bridesmaid," or flip through the wedding album cooing over shots of the bridal party. No one adds "bridesmaid" to their résumé under "Education and Experience" or wears a special piece of jewelry to indicate their acceptance into the Bridesmaid Fold. But imagine if they did. Who knows, maybe *The New York Times* Vows section would start giving as much ink to the qualifications of the attendants as they do the betrothed:

Jessica Hardy, Melissa McNamara, and Elise Campbell yesterday stood up for their good friend Monica Richard, who was married at the Lake Serenity Country Club.

The bridesmaids wore $300 pink taffeta dresses that made them look "hippy," and carried bouquets of calla lilies, to which McNamara had an allergic reaction.

Hardy, 27, has known The Bride since childhood. The two grew up together in the suburbs of Connecticut and swore to be friends forever. Hardy is the daughter of Mr. and Mrs. Stanley Hardy, who were not invited to the ceremony because The Bride's father finds them tiresome.

McNamara, 28, met The Bride when they both attended Vassar College. A political strategist in Washington, D.C., she graduated magna cum laude and saw her dissertation published in the journal *Foreign Affairs*. At the wedding reception, guests repeatedly asked if she was "next."

Campbell, 27, went to camp with The Bride 12 years ago and has since kept in touch via the occasional letter. She once visited The Bride at college but found the weekend awkward and tedious. Throughout the ceremony she mentally calculated the money she had spent on the occasion, and wished she had bought a ticket to Europe instead.

The bridesmaids' dresses will be burned.

I DO-OVER

A happy bridesmaid makes a happy bride.

—LORD ALFRED TENNYSON

t was not the first time I had found myself with a Bad reputation.

And, as it was with my teenage rep, the designation was not entirely undeserved. But I had been asked to stand as a bridesmaid a second time that summer, in the wedding party of my best friend, and I was terrified that she, too, would kick me out after learning of my Bad behavior.

Maybe I would be issued a lifetime ban, I worried, a Bridesmaid Red Card retiring me from professional play and forcing me back to the minor leagues of wedding attendance, where I would be greeted as just another tipsy guest and nothing more. I was unbondable as a bridesmaid now, a liability, a flight risk, and damaged goods.

Thankfully, my best friend had laughed when I mustered up the nerve to describe to her my attendant shame. In the wisdom gained through years of friendship, she told me that my big mouth had once again landed me in trouble and that I should have seen the whole disaster coming a mile away. She noted that if she had wanted a bridesmaid who was helpful and attentive she would have made another choice from the start. It seems it was not news to her that my respect for tradition and ability to behave like an adult left something to be desired.

I sighed with relief and silently vowed to be the Best Bridesmaid the world had ever seen.

They say that opposites attract, but this is not the case when it comes to a successful union of bride and bridesmaid. I believe that things went smoothly in my best friend's wedding because she was as stunned by the process as I was, amazed that she would be wearing white and dedicating her life to a single man. She, too, was shocked that a cake could have a three-digit price tag and that a venue must be booked fourteen months in advance. Each step toward the aisle was a novel form of entertainment for both of us, as odd and unexpected as if she had decided to join the circus. When it came to doing what was expected, she was something of a Bad Bride herself.

It had been this way since the beginning. When she came home from a New Zealand vacation engaged, she and her fiancé had listened to me blab on for an hour over drinks before they mentioned their own exciting news. She did her best to maintain her taste and tact throughout her engagement, which was—mercifully—just eight months long. She wanted to be married, not mired in wedding planning, and refused to drag the whole thing out. She was excited, yes, but wanted to throw the ultimate party—not a pristine event—and for her, this meant killer food, good music, and the rental of a large lakefront home where the bridal party, her siblings, and other friends could stay to prolong the festivities into the wee hours.

As she prepared to get hitched in her own particular style, she accepted my contributions—however minimal—with grace and humor, even when I appeared at her engagement party with a gift-wrapped copy of *The Meaning of Wife*, a book that examines the misogyny and materialism of marriage. I was not scolded and told that feminism has no place at a wedding celebration. Instead, the bride and groom laughed, and guests took turns reading sections of the tome aloud as we stood around the bar.

When we went dress shopping with her mother and the other bridesmaids, she was clear that she didn't care what we wore, as long as we were happy and comfortable. She had our backs when we entered one bridal store and found rack after rack of awful dresses, their shiny fabrics glowing under the sallow lighting, their seams already showing signs of distress from the weekends of women who had reluctantly pulled them on.

We gamely retired to the dressing room and when we reemerged, the MOB did her best to be supportive, politely commenting on flattering aspects of our looks while diplomatically suggesting that perhaps hot pink floor-length was not the way to go. The Bride, however, was nowhere to be seen. I walked outside in my Vegas showgirl number and found her sitting on a bench, head in hands. "That place is horrible," she said. "We're leaving right now."

For her bachelorette party we adopted what we were told was a French bridal tradition called *enterrement de jeune fille*—funeral of a young woman—placing photographs and mementos of our friendship into a small casket that another friend had found at a neighborhood Goth store. The Bride loved the tribute, and carried the black box under one arm as we bar-hopped and danced the night away, even proudly displaying it on the plastic tablecloth of a Chinese restaurant where we went for late-night greasy food to soak up all the booze.

There were many pre-wedding events, but she went out of her way to make them unimposing and optional. She told me that I didn't have to come to the linen party thrown in her honor, probably because she knew I would say something inappropriate about what she was going to do on her new seven-hundred-thread-count sheets.

Because she maintained her perspective and her sense of humor about the endeavor, I actually found myself wanting to do more to help. I pored through books of poetry when she mentioned her desire to have a work of literature included in her ceremony, marveling at how sexually explicit Margaret Atwood could be and wondering if Tupac's verse had ever been read aloud in a Protestant church. I transcribed Maya Angelou and memorized Shakespeare sonnets before she settled on "Dance Me to the End of Love" by Leonard Cohen, a perfect last-minute find.

When my bridesmaid dress was finished, I rushed it home before she could have a change of heart, and was so determined to look halfway decent in it that I even bought a pair of Spanx to wear underneath. The tiny tube of stretch material looked like a bandage you would be given for a sprained ankle or wrist, and I seriously doubted that I would be able to pull it over one foot, let alone the length of my body, from chest to knee.

As anyone who has had the misfortune to wear a pair of Spanx knows, putting the thing on is as traumatic—if not more so—as just letting it all hang out. The elasticized material is supposed to smooth out all your bumps, but that means you have to cram them in there first. I had imagined the Spanx molding my figure into an entirely different formation, that my thighs would be pushed backward into a Jennifer Lopez–like butt, my belly flattened in a nonsurgical tuck, and all excess flesh miraculously relocated to my chest.

In the end, it didn't make any difference at all. When the wedding day came, I looked exactly the same as I had without the full-body suction device, other than the fact that the Spanx peeked out from under my cocktail-length dress like a pair of ribbed beige leggings. But you can't say I didn't try.

This is not to say there weren't moments when I silently cursed my luck or marveled at the things that can trip a girl up on her way down the aisle.

On the beautiful September afternoon before the wedding, I made my way out of town for the rehearsal dinner, only to find myself stuck in bumper-to-bumper traffic. Somehow, a man had managed to drive his car underneath a tractor trailer, wedging it there and stopping traffic on four lanes of busy rush-hour highway.

As my companion and I waited for emergency services to pull the driver (who survived) and his car (which did not) out from under the truck, the traffic jam turned into a makeshift tailgate party. Men and their sons tossed footballs around, women read magazines in the front seat and filed their nails to pass the time, and everyone tried to deal with the inconvenience as calmly as possible. Except for me. I drank warm beer out of a case in the trunk and momentarily considered hitching a ride with a lecherous long-haul driver, who yelled filthy pickup lines at me from the collector lane, which was still slowly inching forward on the other side of the highway median.

I could not be late for this rehearsal, I told myself over and over again, and I would risk abduction at the hands of a mesh hat–wearing redneck before I allowed myself to add to my permanent record as a Bad Bridesmaid. I was not going to miss my shot at redemption because some idiot had mistaken a moving truck for a fast-food drive-through window.

Four hours later, having rejected the offer of a ride from Mr. HOW'S MY DRIVING? CALL 1-800-SCREW YOU, we pulled into the parking lot of a picturesque country church and I leapt from the passenger seat, spilling out along with crumpled cigarette packages and empty beer bottles. I sprinted from the car and slammed through the doors of the church, expecting to see the rehearsal in full swing, the officiant rolling his eyes at my tardiness, and a basin of holy water sizzling at my very presence. Instead, there was no one there. I had been phoning my friend The Bride almost constantly, but she was sitting calmly on a lakeside dock with her family, and returned my call just minutes after I dashed into the empty church. She informed me that I must have confused the time of the rehearsal with the hour the ceremony would begin the next day.

I was an hour early.

There were other disasters narrowly averted. On the morning of the ceremony, The Bride realized that she had left time for everything except writing her own vows, and we spent some time in a tearful huddle before I convinced her that no one can really hear that stuff anyway.

The wedding photographer came equipped with canisters of film, unaware that even blind grandmothers are now shooting digital. When it appeared The Bride was going to shove a roll of film up his slow-winding ass, I ran to the martini bar and fetched her a drink, helping calm her nerves between motorized clicks.

When the newlyweds realized they had forgotten the CD with her first dance song on it at their cottage, I pried her younger brother away from the attractive female guests long enough to make him drive back and get it.

And during the speeches, one of the flower girls climbed onto my lap for a better view. She was four and adorable, and I enjoyed the fact that she somehow sensed we were in this together. When she offered me a stick of lip gloss, I slid it across my mouth, thinking how cute it

was that she had brought her own makeup kit to participate in the grown-up event.

"I found it on the floor," she told me when I had
smacked my lips together.

For a moment, I contemplated tossing her off my lap
and gargling with champagne, but instead I laughed and
chalked it up to karma.

After it was all over, I was actually amazed at how little
I had to do. Part of me had wanted to make a speech or
lead the room in a toast, or at least hold The Bride's flowers while she traded rings.

The logic of women is a mysterious thing, and we often
find ourselves craving roles, men, and carbohydrates we
had once resolutely shunned. Women who plan nontradi-
tional weddings still want it known that they have friends
willing to parade around in a silly outfit for them. And
some of us really do try to be good wedding attendants
even though we are bad at taking orders and not being the
center of attention.

Two months earlier, I had spent the duration of a wedding trying to disappear into my own skin. After successfully making it down the aisle in wedding number two, I
found myself thinking instead about Daisy Leach, a
ninety-two-year-old British woman who had been a
bridesmaid earlier in the year for her forty-five-year-old
niece. The *Financial Times* had reported that Mrs. Leach
was supposed to have been a bridesmaid more than sev-
enty years earlier, at the wedding of her brother George in
1929. Two days before the special event, Daisy's sister Flo-
rie, who was just nineteen, was killed on her way to work
at Harrod's department store, when a car hit her bicycle.
The wedding went ahead as planned, but the devastated
Mrs. Leach did not participate.

Decades later, she told her niece, Gillian Curtis, that she had always wanted to be a bridesmaid, and was granted her request in the form of a blue-and-pink dress and lilac-colored hat.

"My great aunt was absolutely delighted when we asked her," Gillian told the media. "I suppose her dream of becoming a bridesmaid has come true."

I thought about Daisy as I stood at altar left during my best friend's wedding. From where I was positioned, I could see the expression on her face as she repeated her vows and watch her slide a ring onto her new husband's finger. As the rest of the church watched the priest and admired the back of The Bride's veil, I actually saw her get married, the happiness on her face, and the sparkle in her eyes as she prepared to seal it with a kiss. Bridesmaids have a unique perspective on the weddings they attend, and like Daisy, I wouldn't have given up a second shot at that view for the world.

Not every bridesmaid will make it to that special place without some misfortune, without rolling her eyes or questioning the emotional toll or expense of it all. Most women who take on the role, however, do so out of sincere happiness for their friend and the desire to share their special day. "I love her to death, but . . ." they would say to me before launching into their stories of bridesmaid hell.

Like me, they all wanted to be a part of the event, dancing and drinking and sending their friend off to her new married life in style.

A lot of us bridesmaids really do our best to be Good in the name of her big day.

But sometimes it's just so much easier to be Bad.

ACKNOWLEDGMENTS

A big thank-you to all the women who contributed stories for this book.

My literary agent, Rick Broadhead, who is all business even without a cell phone, and who knows more about bridesmaids than any man should. Sarah Knight, Patrick Clark, and everyone at Henry Holt. Iris Tupholme, Kate Cassaday, Melanie Storoschuk, and the team at HarperCollins, for supporting the book from the beginning and keeping me in line to the end.

Steve Meurice, John Racovali, Doug Kelly, Sarah Murdoch, Anne Marie Owens, and everyone at the *National Post* for being the funniest people in journalism.

Chloé Raincock, Elizabeth McGroarty, Jenna Greck, Aynsley Toole, Sarah Redekopp, Jessica Johnson, Gillian Hnatiw, Maggie Wente, and Amy O'Brian—the coolest girl-friends a chick can have.

Beth Montemurro, Cele Otnes, Deborah McCoy, and Jennifer Whidden for their insight on all things wedding related.

Kazuyoshi Ehara and Jordana Huber for dealing with my hatred of cameras.

The McGinn and Garcia families for their support.

My family—Tina, Michael, and Kirsty Agrell—for loving me even when I'm bad.

And thanks to brides everywhere, because we really do love you.

ABOUT THE AUTHOR

SIRI AGRELL is a reporter and columnist with Canada's *National Post* and primarily covers cultural trends. She has written articles on everything from fashion and politics to the pope and those crazy Bush twins. She lives in Toronto.